how to get your

e·Book

published

an insider's
guide to the
world of
electronic
publishing

Richard Curtis
and William Thomas Quick

W

WRITER'S DIGEST BOOKS
CINCINNATI, OHIO

www.writersdigest.com

"If Information Wants to Be Free . . . Then Who's Going to Pay for It?" reprinted with permission from Richard T. Kaser, Vice President, Content Information Today, Inc.

"How to Choose an Editorial Service" reprinted with permission from Susan Mary Malone, author, owner, Malone Editorial Services (www.maloneeditorial.com).

Material excerpted from the Writer Beware Web site on subsidy, vanity and print-on-demand publishers reprinted with permission from Victoria Strauss. Strauss is the author of five fantasy novels, most recently *The Garden of the Stone* (HarperCollins Eos). She is an active member of the Science Fiction and Fantasy Writers of America, where she serves as vice-chair of the Writing Scams Committee and maintains the Writer Beware literary scams warning Web site (www.sfwa.org/beware/).

How to Get Your E-Book Published. Copyright © 2002 by Richard Curtis and William Thomas Quick. Manufactured in the United States of America. All rights reserved. No part of this book may be reproduced in any form or by any electronic or mechanical means including information storage and retrieval systems without permission in writing from the publisher, except by a reviewer, who may quote brief passages in a review. Published by Writer's Digest Books, an imprint of F&W Publications, Inc., 4700 East Galbraith Road, Cincinnati, Ohio 45236. (800) 289-0963. First edition.

Visit our Web site at www.writersdigest.com for information on more resources for writers.

To receive a free weekly e-mail newsletter delivering tips and updates about writing and about Writer's Digest products, register directly at our Web site at http://newsletters.fwp ublications.com.

06   05   04   03   02   5   4   3   2   1

Library of Congress Cataloging-in-Publication Data

Curtis, Richard.
   How to get your e-book published / by Richard Curtis and William Thomas Quick.
    p.   cm.
   Includes bibliographical references and index.
   ISBN 1-58297-095-5 (alk. paper)—ISBN 1-58297-097-1 (pbk.: alk. paper)
    1. Electronic publishing. 2. Self-publishing. 3. Electronic books. 4. Authorship—Marketing. I. Quick, W.T. II. Title.

Z286.E43 C87   2002
070.57'97—dc21   2001046827
                                                    CIP

Edited by Donya Dickerson
Designed by Sandy Conopeotis Kent
Cover by Beckmeyer Design, Cincinnati, OH
Production coordinated by Kristen Heller

DEDICATION

From Richard Curtis:

To Leslie, my steadfast companion through p-books and e-books

From William Thomas Quick:

To Desmond Mong Seng Tan

Richard Curtis

PHOTO BY LESLIE CURTIS

Late in 1998, Richard Curtis announced the formation of e-reads, a publisher dedicated to reissuing, in e-book and print formats, previously published books in such popular categories as romance, fantasy, science fiction and thriller. The company commenced operation in 1999 with over 1,200 titles, many by famous names in their fields, and concluded strategic alliances with a dozen major distributors including Amazon.com, Barnes & Noble and Ingram Book Company. In addition to running e-reads, Curtis is also president of Richard Curtis Associates, Inc., a leading New York literary agency which currently represents close to 150 authors in such categories of fiction as romance, western, thriller, science fiction and fantasy.

His books include *How to Be Your Own Literary Agent, Beyond the Bestseller, Mastering the Business of Writing* and *This Business of Publishing.* He has testified as an expert witness in several publishing trials.

He was the first president of the Independent Literary Agents Association and was President of the Association of Authors' Representatives in 1996 and 1997. His company served for over a decade as agency for the Science Fiction and Fantasy Writers of America. In 1994, he received the prestigious Romance Writers of America Industry Award for Distinguished Service to Authors. In 1999, he was invited to serve on the editorial advisory board of *Writer's Digest.* In 2000, he was invited to serve on the advisory board for the publishing Master in Science program at Pace University.

William Thomas Quick

William Thomas Quick is a futurist, a science fiction author of more than thirty books, a screenwriter and the owner of Iceberg SOHO Systems, a small business network consulting firm. His story "Bank Robbery," published in *Analog Science Fiction and Fact* magazine in 1989, accurately predicted the upheaval the World Wide Web would create in the world of traditional publishing several years before the e-book revolution began.

TABLE OF CONTENTS

WELCOME TO THE FUTURE: AN INTRODUCTION TO ELECTRONIC PUBLISHING

GUTENBERG'S WORLD

Five hundred fifty years ago, Johannes Gutenberg introduced the printing press to Europe and created the basic publishing model that has existed with little change into the present day.

That model is simple: Writers write, then sell their work to publishers.

Publishers print the work, distribute it, promote it, sell it and pay the writers a small fee, or "royalty," on each book sold.

Gutenberg invented the printing press, but you still had to own one to be a publisher. Gutenberg himself died a poor man, even though his invention changed the world forever.

Gutenberg's world, which had remained essentially unaltered for more than half a millennium, started changing in the early 1990s with the advent of a strange technological place called the Internet. At that time the "Net" was a small, sickly world of flickering green letters on tiny black screens, inhabited mostly by people much of the world thought of as geeks—or worse.

Even so, there were people—people just like you—who saw the potential of the medium as a new way of publishing. Project Gutenberg, created in 1971 by a visionary named Michael Hart, began to "digitize" small but well-known public domain texts like the *Declaration of Independence* and make them available without charge to anybody on the Net. Other writers posted their work in discussion groups on Usenet, a collection of Internet "bulletin boards."

INNOVATORS OF THE DIGITAL REVOLUTION

- **Tim Berners-Lee:** Invented the World Wide Web.
- **Robert Cailliau:** Along with Berners-Lee, invented the Web browser.
- **Michael Hart:** First to send e-texts across a network; founder of the Gutenberg Project.

From such inauspicious beginnings came a revolution that is only now reaching its first fruition. In the early 1990s, courtesy of Tim Berners-Lee of CERN (the European Organization for Nuclear Research), a new kind of Net called the World Wide Web made its appearance—and changed everything. Computer technology had advanced enough that many people had large computer screens capable of color, which were tailor-made for the new Web medium. A piece of software called a "Web browser" (invented by Berners-Lee and Robert Cailliau) allowed people to view "Web pages," which resembled the pages of a glossy paper magazine. You could put *anything* on those Web pages, and *anybody in the world* could come and look at your work. In effect, anybody could become a publisher, and not only that, a publisher whose potential market was the entire world. Thus was born "electronic publishing," or "e-publishing," which will eventually be recognized as the greatest revolution in publishing since Johannes Gutenberg's invention of the printing press.

It has been said that freedom of the press is for those who own one. The electronic age puts a "digital printing press" into the hands of anyone who owns a computer and has access to the Internet.

That means into *your* hands. This book is your operations manual for that press.

Welcome to the revolution. Again.

PART ONE

Understanding the Power and Potential of E-Publishing

CHAPTER ONE

THE FIRST STEPS TOWARD E-PUBLISHING

T he letter "e" has been stuck onto the front of so many different words—somewhat like pinning all-purpose tails on the noses of a herd of donkeys—that it has become somewhat nebulous in meaning. For the average person, the "e" prefix means the modified item has something to do with technology or, more specifically, the Internet. And so we get everything from "e-tailing" (a play on "retailing," usually referring to peddling something from a Web page over the Internet) to notions as bizarre as "e-wear," referring to clothing that has computers built into it.

It is the nebulousness of the definition that makes real understanding of e-publishing difficult to attain. A more accurate term

FIVE SIMPLE STEPS TO E-PUBLICATION

- Write your book.
- Convert it to digital format.
- Get connected to the Internet.
- Build a Web page.
- Transfer the book to your Web page and make it available for viewing or download.

would be "d-publishing," where the "d" stands for "digital." For the purpose of this book, we will define "e-publishing" as "publishing books in digital format" and "e-books" as "literary works in digital format."

Michael Hart, creator of the Gutenberg Project (http://promo .net/pg/) and one of the giant early figures of electronic publishing, provides a further gloss on this when he writes: "E-books are the physical machine reading devices. E-texts are what you read on them. . . ." This is a distinction well worth keeping in mind. The map is not the territory.

E-publishing allows for a host of presentation media; and in this book, we will examine those already in existence, those planned for the immediate future and even some notions that may or may not come to fruition.

In the Beginning Is the Word

In the beginning, you must write. You must create the information. You must move from the idea to the concrete and specific creation that only you can do. Everything in the large and changing structure of electronic publishing depends on this all-important fact: Without the content, the information, the *work*, nothing else can exist. In order to publish, market, distribute, first you must have *something* to do it all with.

The famous film producer Irving Thalberg is reputed to have said, in 1939, that, "The writer is the most important person in Hollywood, but we must never tell the sons of bitches." What Thalberg was acknowledging (and what Hollywood often goes to great lengths to conceal or ignore) is that no movie can be made until a script has been written.

In similar fashion, no book has ever been published until a manuscript has been created by a writer. While, for the uninitiated, writing may seem a simple, almost negligible, talent, *good* writing is hard to do. As the legendary journalist Gene Fowler said, "Writing is easy; all you do is sit staring at a blank sheet of paper until the drops of blood form on your forehead."

Today, of course, many writers no longer stare at a blank sheet of paper, but an empty computer screen is no less daunting, and the blood continues to flow, only this time it's computer keyboards that get all sticky.

So, first you must write. Dorothy Parker once said, "I hate writing, but I love having written." You have to write, and you must reach the point of "having written." Once you've done that, e-publishing can play a role in the next stage of your creation.

CHAPTER TWO

A FEW WORDS FROM THE AUTHORS

William T. Quick

It has now been just a hair more than forty years since that day early in my high school years when I made up my mind, once and for all, about what I wanted to do with the rest of my life. I decided I was going to be a writer.

Unlike most such decisions (Remember when you just *knew* that being a cowboy was the only way to go?), mine actually panned out; and I now find myself, millions of words later, doing exactly what I planned to do all those years ago. I have few regrets, but I have to confess that at times I am reminded of the old proverb, "Be careful what you wish for. You might just get it."

Like a lot of writers who finally manage to make a living at this game, I wrote hundreds of thousands of "practice" words before I sold anything at all. During that time, I paid my bills doing lots of things—one of which, in 1965, was computer programming. Back in those days, a computer was the size of a small railroad car, and the notion of putting one on a desk seemed downright ridiculous. In those days, the Internet—or any kind of computer network, for that matter—didn't exist.

Still, if you were a budding science fiction writer—and I was—the potential of these great, ungainly digital beasts was intriguing. And so began my love-hate affair with all things computer, which, like my writing, has persisted to this day.

In the mideighties, I walked into a Radio Shack and bought a miracle, or at least it seemed like one to me. It was a computer a thousand times more powerful than that room-sized hunk of glass and steel on which I'd first learned to program. Not only that, it cost about ten thousand times less, I could lift it without a crane and, yes, I could put it on my desk. I became a foot soldier in the digital revolution, where I have marched ever since.

The confluence of these two passions—writing and computers—led me to write a story in 1987 about how networks of personal computers might affect the publishing business. That story, "Bank Robbery," published in *Analog Science Fiction and Fact*, told the tale of an editor made jobless by the collapse of the print publishing business. He created a new career for himself trolling in cyberspace for talented new writers and helping them to develop their skills and "publishing" their work on the "world network."

Not bad guesswork on my part, given that the World Wide Web had yet to be invented. My mutually entwined interests continued apace, as I thought about, wrote about and worked with the shiny new toys of the digital age.

Eventually, I ended up self-publishing my own work in small "critical" editions, using programs like Microsoft Word and Adobe FrameMaker to create and format digital books, then printing them out and hand-binding them myself. I learned to build Web pages and headed up a project that e-published Jack Mingo's famous *Whole Pop Catalog* in 1995 as an interactive Web site—one of the first of its type. My latest wrinkle is to see my backlist of out-of-print books now being reissued as e-books, as well as in print-on-demand format.

A Few Words From the Authors

In other words, I've been around a long time, both as a writer and as a participant in the digital revolution that is sweeping through traditional publishing. As writers, we live in challenging but exciting times. The standard verities of publishing are starting to crumble, but the full shape of the future is not yet clearly in our vision. Yet we can see clearly enough: Tools and methods already exist that allow you to create and publish your writing in ways undreamed of even ten years ago.

Learn From My Experiences

As the geek half of this writing collaboration, I've done the hands-on research into software, hardware and all the other digital trinkets you can use to e-publish your writing. Over the past twenty years I've made plenty of mistakes as I stumbled, sometimes painfully, into this new age. Much of what you'll read in this book is a distillation of all my trial and error, my failures and successes, into a set of methods and tools that can be as simple, or as complicated, as you desire. Be assured, though: Whether simple or complicated, these tools and methods will be more powerful—and liberating—than anything you've ever used before.

Some of you may find e-publishing daunting. But it need not be so. Five years ago, my friend, agent and coauthor of this book, Richard Curtis, was not even connected to the Internet. Today, he is a "netpreneur," founder of his own e-publishing company, an advocate for writers' e-rights and a major force in the digital publishing revolution that is rapidly expanding the boundaries for all writers everywhere in the world.

But I'll let him speak for himself . . .

Richard Curtis

I've been called a lot of names, but "geek" is definitely not one of them. I could not program a single line of code if the fate of humanity depended on it. Yet, I have educated myself enough so that when I talk to technical people I can sling around "XML," "PDF," "JPEG" and "gigs of RAM" with the best of 'em. I just secretly pray that they won't ask me for details! Besides, I respect them too much to call them geeks. Their genius is transforming the rusty relic of twentieth-century publishing into a streamlined, powerful and blazingly fast machine capable of delivering books from the author's imagination to the reader's mind in the blink of an eye.

Had anyone told me in the early 1990s that I would be in the information technology business, I would not even have understood what the letters "I.T." stood for. I did know that a revolution was brewing, though. Early in the 1980s, I began writing a column in *Locus*, a science fiction trade publication, interpreting trends in the publishing industry for the magazine's readers. Around 1989 I began to hear about portable electronic devices capable of displaying entire books, devices that functioned like desktop computers. I rushed out for a demonstration, and crude as those Franklin Electronic Bibles and dictionaries were, I knew in a flash that it was only a matter of time before dedicated handheld electronic readers would become commonplace. I predicted it in one of my gee-whiz columns, but no one paid much attention. It was after all a science fiction publication, and "cyberbooks" had been showing up in SF books for years.

But I couldn't stop thinking about the revolutionary implications of those gadgets, and I kept wondering what role I might play when the revolution struck. It was clear that whatever the application of the computer might be, it tended to "disintermediate" the relationship between seller and buyer, that is, eliminate all the middlemen and women necessary to deliver a product from the former to the latter. Now, a literary agent is nothing if not a middleman, so if the process applied to the product known as books, I might very well wake up one day to discover my profession was no longer relevant.

A Few Words From the Authors

By the same logic, however, publishers and bookstores might also become irrelevant. Of course, nobody wants to hear this. When I told a gathering of publishing people that the publishing process could be reduced to the simple formula of "a writer, a reader and a server," you would think I had made a rude noise during a religious service.

Making Prophecies Come True

Nevertheless, I decided that, unlike most prophets, I wanted to get rich from my prophecies. So, as the 1990s progressed, my agency began an aggressive campaign to recover the rights to out-of-print titles by its clients. In 1998 the revolution came in the form of the introduction of two handheld reading devices, the Rocket eBook and the SoftBook Reader. I was ready for it with five hundred books owned lock, stock and barrel by their authors.

But the idea of handling these books in the old-fashioned agent's way wasn't compatible with my vision of this brave new world. That's when I conceived the idea of publishing them myself through my e-reads program. For an agent to become a publisher was unheard of. An author chat room correspondent spread the word that "Curtis has gone over to the dark side." My clients were supportive, however. They held the rights to all these books that might never again see the light of day—what did they have to lose? My model of business was also quite radical: to pay the author 50 percent of all the revenue my publishing company received. Of course, that model is now becoming the gold standard in the e-book industry. I don't mind taking the credit for that!

That is the genesis of e-reads, and though I am laughably far from getting rich by implementing my dream, I have demonstrated that the business model I conceived works. As of this writing, books published in the e-reads program are sold through more than a dozen online and traditional distributors including our own Web site, http://ereads.com, and the royalties earned by these authors increase steadily.

Though the revolution has just begun, it has already thrown the book business into turmoil as young, computer-oriented people "repurpose" it and send it in exciting new directions. Writers have not escaped the repurposing process. Yesterday we called them authors. Today we call them content providers. But don't worry about the nomenclature. Your role is unchanged: The content you provide is the stuff of your imagination, your dreams, your heart and soul. But now you have the means of delivering that stuff to readers in wondrous new ways. I hope this book will help you understand what those ways are and how you can take advantage of them to advance your career.

CHAPTER THREE

THE ROOTS OF E-PUBLISHING

The first question you might ask is, "What good is having a knowledge of the 'ancient' history of technology that led up to the revolutionary opportunities that we, as writers and e-publishers, now enjoy?"

The answer isn't entirely straightforward, but we think it makes sense. To explain, we'll use an anology. Cookbooks give you recipes, step-by-step methods of cooking a dish.

If a recipe needs to be changed, the amateur cook is at a loss without understanding the properties of various ingredients.

The Internet, and the digital revolution, are like gigantic cookbooks whose "recipes" are constantly changing.

Without understanding the history and properties of computers and the Internet, the would-be e-publisher might easily be baffled by even small changes in individual recipes: new software, new standards, new tools that change the field at large.

A solid understanding of *why* computers and the Internet have become the way they are will help you even if some specific e-publishing recipes in this book change or become obsolete. Knowing the history of the field will give you the understanding you need to roll with the punches.

The current changes shaking the foundations of traditional publishing are dependent on and grounded in two things: the power of personal computers and the Internet.

In other words, these are the two areas *you* need to understand fully in order to be a successful e-publisher. To take the notion further, we think you need to understand at least some of the history of technology in order to make sense of the questions currently roiling the e-publishing scene, of debates that deal with the types of software and hardware that will end up as standards or of the wide range of text presentation formats. All of this affects you as a writer and e-publisher; and by providing you with a snapshot of the relevant history, we think we can help you to make better decisions along the path to being an e-publisher.

E-Publishing

If you loosely define "e-publishing" as the publication in digital form of a written work, either on the Internet or in digital format (chips, CDs, etc.), then it is impossible to determine the *precise* moment of the first e-publication. However, the first formal effort at such publication is generally agreed to be the creation of Project Gutenberg by Michael Hart in 1971.

At this time, the Internet as we know it did not exist; instead, something called ARPAnet, the Advanced Research Projects Agency Network, consisting of fewer than fifty computers, was still in its fledgling stages. The computer Hart worked on, a Xerox Sigma 5 mainframe, was one of the machines on this network. As part of his training program, Hart was given $100,000,000 worth of computing time to use as he saw fit. He tried to figure out how he could possibly repay this investment. According to the history of Project Gutenberg (http://promo.net/pg/history.html#beginning) it took him exactly one hour and forty-seven minutes to figure out an answer.

Hart told his fellow operators that "the greatest value created by computers would not be computing, but would be the storage, retrieval, and searching of what was stored in our libraries." He then "proceeded to type in the *Declaration of Independence* and tried to send it to everyone on the networks."

It is fair to say that this was not only the beginning of the legendary Project Gutenberg but the first instance of true e-publishing as well.

E-Mail and Word Processors

From its advent in 1971, electronic publishing primarily involved entering text into a computer and either placing it on a server where others could come to access and read it or sending it by e-mail (also invented in 1971, by Ray Tomlinson, for use on ARPAnet) to other interested parties.

DIGITAL PUBLISHING MILESTONES

- **1971**: First e-texts sent across networks by Michael Hart.
- **1971**: E-mail invented by Ray Tomlinson.
- **1976**: Prototype word processor invented by Michael Shrayer.
- **1976**: Steve Wozniak and Steve Jobs invent the Apple computer.
- **1978**: WordStar, the first successful commercial word processor invented by Seymour Rubenstein, Rob Barnaby and Jim Fox.
- **1981**: IBM introduces the IBM Personal Computer.
- **1985**: Stewart Brand creates the WELL.
- **1991**: Tim Berners-Lee invents the World Wide Web.
- **1992**: One million computers hooked up to the Internet.

But text entry in those days, at least by our standards, was a crude and difficult task. The things we take for granted today—choice of fonts, automatic formatting, easy layout, spell and grammar checking—did not exist. The next major advance in electronic publishing occurred in 1978, with the release of the first commercially successful word processing program for microcomputers called WordStar.

There were earlier word processors, adapted from the line editors programmers used to write their programs. An Altair programmer named Michael Shrayer wrote computer manuals on his computer and in 1976 created the first formal word processing program for the microcomputer, Electric Pencil. His invention did enjoy some popularity but never achieved commercial viability.

In 1978, Seymour Rubenstein left his marketing job at IMS Associates, a maker of personal computers, to found MicroPro International with $8500 of his own money. He brought with him an IMS programmer named Rob Barnaby, and in 1978 Barnaby wrote the first version of WordStar for the CP/M operating system. His assistant, Jim Fox, then rewrote the program to run on MS-DOS in 1981.

WordStar's advent and widespread acceptance revolutionized the task of writing. By allowing the use of fonts, the ability to automatically format text and, most particularly, vastly improved ease of correction and editing, it made the composition, preparation and presentation of texts much simpler than had previously been possible with typewriters and pen or pencil. Even more important, computer word processors automatically created text in digital format—that is, a format that could be used by any digital computer. This was the true genesis of mass electronic publishing.

Famed science fiction author Arthur C. Clarke had this to say about WordStar, on meeting Rubenstein and Barnaby: "I am happy to greet the geniuses who made me a born-again writer; having announced my retirement in 1978, I now have six books in the works and two probables, all through WordStar" (www.inventors.about.com/science/inventors/library/weekly/aa030199.htm). And lucky for you, word processing programs have improved even more since Clarke spoke these words.

WordStar went on to dominate the market for word processors through the late 1980s, until it was supplanted by WordPerfect, but in that time it changed the way much of the writing in the

United States was done and was instrumental in creating the first large body of digitized text in history. One can, to this day, by poking around in dusty corners and forgotten byways of the Internet, discover literary works first created on this early word processor. In fact, one of the authors of this book wrote his first published novel, a science fiction cyberpunk epic called *Dreams of Flesh and Sand*, in 1985 on a version of WordStar running on an early Radio Shack personal computer—and immediately retired the creaky Underwood portable typewriter on which he'd done all his previous work.

Computers at Home

The next important advance in electronic publishing was the rapid expansion of personal computer ownership among the public, fueled by the entry of IBM into the world of personal computing.

In late 1981, IBM introduced the IBM/PC—the "PC" stood for "personal computer," which led to the popularization of that now ubiquitous term. Its immediate success began the process of mass acceptance of such machines, eventually lowering the price of personal computers into the realm of affordability for large numbers of users.

Throughout the 1980s, technology continued to improve, as well as lessen in cost, but one aspect of publishing was still lacking in the digital world: distribution. Thanks to computers and word processors, writers could write more easily and quickly and create work in digitized format as well. But the mainstream publishing houses still had a lock on the most important aspect of writing for the professional writer: They controlled the channels of distribution, marketing and sales. Writers could create literary works, but if they hoped to sell them in such a way as to reach a large public audience, they still had to deal with the publishing houses, which had the only entry into bookstores that actually retailed books.

In large part, this is still the way most publishing is done. But, as you read through this book, you'll see it is no longer the way *all* publishing is done.

Enter the Internet, a Place for Writers From the Start

Today, the Internet is a vast network of computers of all types, connected by various links that allow these machines to "talk" to each other. By the late 1980s, the first outline of what we now have was becoming clear. ARPAnet had become DARPAnet (ARPAnet with the word "defense" in front of it) and had exceeded 100,000 connected computers, primarily on college campuses and government research installations. But it was getting ready to burst out of its academic/government confines into widespread use by the public. In 1985, the Whole Earth 'Lectronic Link, the WELL, was created by Stewart Brand and Larry Brilliant, foreshadowing the model that would eventually become commonplace the world over.

The WELL began primarily as a place for writers and readers, and much of literary nature was exchanged, argued over and maintained electronically as a permanent part of the WELL's electronic history and archives.

By 1992, the number of host computers on the Internet passed the one million mark and has never looked back. Today, computers connected to the Internet number well over a hundred million, and those able to access the Internet make up an even larger group. The last piece of the electronic publishing puzzle was finally in place: a very large potential market and a way to reach them electronically.

The World Wide Web Revolutionizes Publishing

The next major advance that concerns those interested in electronic publishing was the creation of the World Wide Web. Prior to the invention of the browsers and protocols that allow the Web to exist, the Internet was not especially user-friendly. Some familiarity with arcane and unwieldy programs like TIN (for reading Usenet newsgroups) or PINE (an online word processor) were necessary in order to use the Internet.

Further, what most people saw on their computer screens was brutally basic: black and white (or black and green, black and yellow) text. It was possible to send text and picture files that looked better back and forth, but one couldn't simply use the computer to view the literary work of others in the sort of formats we'd become used to in the world of paper and print.

The World Wide Web changed all that and removed the very last proprietary advantage of print: the ability to present writing in any imaginable visual format. In fact, the WWW went beyond print, allowing the creation of literary works and their presentation in ways paper could not duplicate: the inclusion of sound files, for instance, or the ability to link from one document to another with the click of a mouse. Writers could even create "interactive" works, which allowed for, or even demanded, the participation of the reader.

Which brings us to the current state of affairs. As technology has continued to improve, prices for equipment and software have come down. The world of electronic publishing has opened to a vast and ever-growing market of potential producers and readers. The prospects for electronic publishing today are nearly beyond comprehension.

Today, if you have a computer and a connection to the Internet, you can create and publish works available to hundreds of millions of people and do so at a cost of pennies. Never before in human history has this ability existed. Thanks to e-publishing, we can all be creators, publishers and consumers with a reach beyond anything ever before imagined.

CHAPTER FOUR

E-BOOK TYPE ONE: HANDHELD READERS

Printed text itself is a sort of code. After all, what is print except a bunch of lines arranged in a certain way on a sheet of paper? Your eyes are the "machines" used to perceive that code, and your brain contains the "software" you use to decode that code back into content your mind can use. In other words, the combination of you, a book and the code make up a complete "content presentation and retrieval system."

As we enter the digital age, not much has changed—except the form that the "book" itself takes. Now, instead of paper, we have computer screens. And right now, there are two general types of "readers" that make use of those screens. Each has advantages and disadvantages, as you shall soon see.

The *hardware reader*, which we discuss in this chapter, is a computer designed as a separate piece of equipment with a single purpose: to present electronic books to you in a form you can hold in your hand.

The *software reader* is a software program that runs on your computer and lets you use that computer and screen to read electronic books. This can include not just e-book reader programs, but also text readers and, especially, Web browsers that display

.html files. We'll discuss this more in chapter five on software e-book readers.

A third way to receive e-books is through *print on demand.* This method does not necessarily involve a computer screen, but instead, let's you print a traditional book from a digital file. We'll discuss this concept more in chapter six.

The huge changes in computer technology of the past thirty years did not go unnoticed by writers or publishers, nor by other interested parties hoping to adapt to and take advantage of these changes. During the past ten years, as the traditional model of print publishing was being at least threatened with massive change, and at worst facing extinction, one debate dominated much of the conversation. The question was simple: Would paper books be completely replaced by electronic books?

That debate continues to rage, and the outcome is by no means certain at this point. In addition to being able to access books on personal computers, a recent innovation in e-publishing, the stand-alone e-book reader, has further complicated this controversy.

Proponents of the notion that e-book readers would do to print books what CDs did to vinyl records found themselves challenged by opponents who delighted in pointing out apparent drawbacks.

ARGUMENT OF THE E-BOOK NAYSAYERS
- "Who is going to take a computer into the bathtub to read a book?"
- "Who wants to read a book on a flickering, fuzzy computer screen?"
- "A paper book costs as little as six or seven bucks, and it lasts for decades. How much does a computer cost?"
- "Paper books don't run out of batteries."
- "Go ahead. Try to make notes on your book-reader screen or stick a bookmark in to mark your place."

True believers in the future of electronic publishing were initially stumped by many of the questions in the list on page 22, all of which revolved around issues of cost and utility.

Eventually, the two groups reached this general consensus: Electronic book readers will not make headway against paper books until several goals are reached.

- E-book readers must become relatively cheap. A viable price point should be somewhere between fifty and a hundred dollars, comparable to the portable tape/CD players.
- The visual reading experience must be at least comparable to that of reading print.
- The reader must be about the same size and weight as a book.
- Battery life must be sufficient to allow for a relatively worry-free reading experience—enough, say, for a transcontinental airline flight at minimum.

Therefore, those who tried to develop e-book readers aimed for these general standards.

Developing the E-Book

The most notable efforts were from two companies: the SoftBook Reader from SoftBook Press and the Rocket eBook from NuvoMedia. Both of these readers were released in 1998 and met with moderate success but have since been absorbed by Gemstar, which markets two models of its own product, the REB1100, with a black-and-white screen, and the REB1200, a color-screen model, through Thompson/RCA.

A second company, Franklin Books, has released a trio of somewhat less expensive models, with the cheapest only a bit more than a hundred dollars. One of the Gemstar models boasts a battery life of forty hours, and their top-end model offers a high-resolution color screen. None of these readers weighs more than two pounds (less than many hardcover books) and most weigh considerably less. The price, however, is not yet competitive with mass-produced single-media players like the Walkman, and in some cases, the screens do not offer a reading experience at all comparable with print.

One new offering with an interesting twist comes from Korea ebook: This company has teamed up with eBookAd.com, an Internet electronic book portal, to offer the hiebook eBook Reader, an extremely lightweight (10.5 ounces), high-resolution reader that promises long battery life and the capability to play MP3 files, games, make recordings and maintain a personal information manager as well as store and read e-books.

A considerable body of people within the e-publishing industry believes that, if stand-alone readers are to survive at all, they will have to be something like the hiebook and offer features beyond simple text reading.

At this point, we can't say with any certainty what the end result of the debate will be or which stand-alone hardware e-reader concept will win out. We suspect, however, that as the cost of computer screens, storage and processing power continues to lessen—and if the history of technology and the Internet teaches us anything, it *will* keep on dropping—then the software e-book reading systems will become more and more viable, running on all-purpose portable computer platforms. And the companies developing readers will continue to consider the wide range of needs of the buying public. In other words, there's a good chance your notebook computer will become your e-book reader as well.

CHAPTER FIVE

E-BOOK TYPE TWO: SOFTWARE E-BOOK READERS

A separate category of electronic book readers uses software programs that, once installed on a computer, turn the computer into a book reader able to display books created in the proprietary formats of the readers.

THE BIG THREE E-PUBLISHING SOFTWARE READER/FORMATS

- Microsoft Reader
- Adobe eBook Reader
- Any Web browser (HTML Format)

The earliest readers, of course, were text editors or word processors. A simple text editor like Microsoft's Notepad or Apple's SimpleText can display any text file for reading. Text files are the lowest common denominator of electronic publishing formats. They are fully portable, which means that almost all computer operating systems offer some way of reading them. For example, text is the format of choice for Project Gutenberg's e-books, since Gutenberg intends to reach the widest possible audience with its offerings.

Books may be created and/or displayed in the formats of other word processors, of course. High-end word processors like Microsoft Word, Corel WordPerfect and StarOffice's StarWriter are capable of creating and displaying works not only in simple text but also in fully formatted text, with an infinite variety of fonts and colors, hypertext links, and even multimedia inclusions like sound or video files. Perhaps most important for those who wish to publish their own work on the Internet, most complete word processors now offer the capability of creating work in the HTML format, which is the standard format for displaying on the World Wide Web.

For those who wish to create material directly for the Web without using an intermediary word processor, there are dozens of choices among what are called "HTML editors." These include:

- Microsoft's FrontPage
- SoftQuad's HoTMetaL PRO
- V-Tech Software's WebMaster
- Netscape's Composer (which is fully integrated into Netscape's Web browser, versions 4.0 or later)
- and many others

All of this software allows a writer to easily prepare work for display on the Web—but not just for the Web alone.

Many e-publishers now choose to offer e-books in HTML format, because all modern computers usually have a Web browser built into their operating systems. These browsers don't have to be connected to the Internet in order to display HTML files. They can read such files directly off a computer's hard drive, which makes HTML as universal a format as plain text.

Finally, there are the dedicated, proprietary format e-book readers mentioned previously. In the past few years, several of these made an appearance, the best known of which were the Glassbook Reader and Adobe's PDF format. Stephen King's groundbreaking

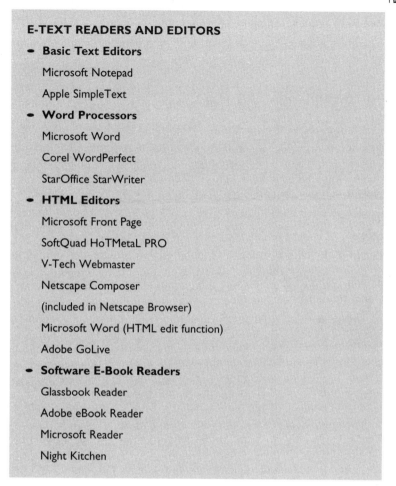

E-TEXT READERS AND EDITORS
- **Basic Text Editors**

  Microsoft Notepad

  Apple SimpleText
- **Word Processors**

  Microsoft Word

  Corel WordPerfect

  StarOffice StarWriter
- **HTML Editors**

  Microsoft Front Page

  SoftQuad HoTMetaL PRO

  V-Tech Webmaster

  Netscape Composer

  (included in Netscape Browser)

  Microsoft Word (HTML edit function)

  Adobe GoLive
- **Software E-Book Readers**

  Glassbook Reader

  Adobe eBook Reader

  Microsoft Reader

  Night Kitchen

Web-distributed story *Riding the Bullet* was offered in the Glassbook format. This novella, which was downloaded hundreds of thousands of times and earned several hundred thousand dollars for its author, stunned the print publishing world by establishing, once and for all, that at least some big-name authors could profitably e-publish their work.

Since Glassbook's rise, Microsoft has entered the fray with its Microsoft Reader application, and Glassbook itself has been ab-

E-Book Type Two: Software E-Book Readers

sorbed by Adobe, creators of the PDF format, which has announced it will integrate Glassbook technology into its own products.

Comparing the Two Methods of Delivery

How do these software readers compare to the handheld readers? Price-wise, there is no contest. Both the Adobe Reader and the Microsoft Reader are free. Both companies have made alliances with large publishing houses and book distributors. The reader can choose among thousands of e-books to buy for these readers and thousands more that are free. Depending on the capabilities of the machine on which they are installed, these readers can also offer greater screen resolution, storage and download speed than the stand-alone e-book readers.

Given these advantages, one might assume there is no reason to use handheld readers. Why spend several hundred dollars to purchase a dedicated e-book reader or why write in formats for such a reader, when you can have a software version that does more and costs nothing?

The answer is security—an important concept for writers. Stand-alone readers are more secure than the software versions. In fact, the question of security is so crucial to the future of electronic publishing itself that we discuss it in greater depth later in this book.

It is fair to say that, as we enter the new millennium, the debate about electronic publishing readers has evolved into two surviving visions: the stand-alone, proprietary electronic reader and the software package that transforms any computer into a book reader. This debate only concerns you if you are interested in creating work you want to *sell* to the general public.

If all you want is to publish your work and place it, free of charge, before the world, there are innumerable excellent ways to go about this, many of which are, for all intents and purposes, free (assuming that one already owns a computer that is connected to the Internet). As an example, you could use a word processor to create a book, then use the same word processor to format the work into HTML, then place the book on a Web site for reading or downloading—using nothing more than the software usually included when you purchased the computer.

But if you harbor the dream of making a living as a writer of electronic books, deciding which models you will use to deliver your book to your readers is of paramount importance. Essentially, the decisions you make as to which reading models you intend to use for your e-book are as critical as the ones book makers have made for millennia as to what sort of paper, bindings and formats (books, scrolls, papyrus sheets, stone) they will publish on.

In fact, one might wistfully note here that print publishers have traditionally enjoyed an advantage over e-publishers because their formats and mediums last for more than a few months. Of course, digital text has been with us nearly half a century now, and it remains a perfectly good format for e-publishing. And even though you may feel that software formats change so fast that it's impossible to keep track of them, they are actually improving and expanding the visual opportunities and delivery methods for your book, which will ultimately help you reach a wider audience. Nevertheless, e-publishing has a way to go before it achieves the longevity of Gutenberg's movable type.

CHAPTER SIX

E-BOOK TYPE THREE: PRINT-ON-DEMAND BOOKS

Print on demand (POD) is one of those notions that is neither fish nor fowl; it partakes of both the digital revolution and the print methods we've used for thousands of years to present words on some sort of tangible medium like paper.

Print on demand is essentially a bridge between a print world and a digital world. In this method of e-publishing, a digital file can be transferred into some sort of computer-screen reader for viewing or it can be fed directly into a computerized printing machine, which will then print on paper as many copies as are wanted—even if only one copy is required. Most books are actually printed from digital files these days, instead of the old method of shooting film of the pages. Even the products of the large print publishers are set in type, not by sweating laborers but by computers operating from file templates already in digital format. So, moving books to a POD format is a natural step.

As writers, we need to accept that there are millions of people alive today who may never read a book on a computer screen. Maybe they just don't like computers, they can't afford them or they just can't imagine reading anything else but a paper book. What print on demand does is allow them to do so, but the *produc-*

tion of that book is drastically altered by the fact that the original content is in digital format.

Benefits of Print on Demand

Print on demand does away with the idea of inventory. Instead of cases of books moldering away in warehouses, your inventory consists of a single digital file, which any "bookmaking" machine can use to crank out a paper book. It also offers some intriguing options for those who love paper books and wish to see the old-style bookstore/bookbuyer model continue. One can easily imagine a neighborhood bookshop with one of these "book printers" in an otherwise empty back room. Out in front, the shelves hold thousands of single copies of individual books the store owner believes her customers will find of interest. Customers still come in, browse through the shelves as they always have, picking up paper books and leafing through them, perhaps reading a paragraph here and there. When the customer finds something he likes, he takes his purchase to the cash register, pays and carries his paper book home to read. The store owner checks his sales records (kept on a computer, no doubt) and makes a decision whether to print out a new copy of the book or perhaps replace it with a copy of something new.

Presto. The customer gets his itch to read something on paper immediately gratified. The owner no longer has to worry about the costs of keeping crates of books in the back room, of buying books that won't sell or returning books that didn't sell. Moreover, the owner has access to a huge inventory at a moment's notice—if somebody comes in and asks for a book that's not on the shelves, the owner merely says, "Wait just one minute," makes a quick trip to the back room and returns with the book in question. No waiting for "special orders," and no such thing as "Sorry, that's no longer in print." It may not be in print—but it can be, given a few seconds of notice.

E-Book Type Three: Print-on-Demand Books

And for those who don't feel the visceral need for the bookstore browsing experience but just want to buy that book right now, there's no reason these printing machines couldn't be scattered about as ubiquitously as ATM machines. Just walk up to one at any time, day or night, shove in your credit card and walk away with your book a few moments later.

All of this because the real book, which is the content that makes up the book, now exists in a form so small and easy to copy into a host of different formats that it makes you wonder: How many books can dance on the head of a pin?

As many as you want, of course.

CHAPTER SEVEN

HOW E-PUBLISHING IS CHANGING HOW BOOKS ARE PUBLISHED

So far, we have touched on methods of reading electronic works. But what about publishing e-books? In fact, what does the word "publish" mean?

> *Definition of Publish:*
> 1. *To prepare and issue (printed material) for public distribution or sale.*
> 2. *To bring to the public attention; announce.*

The second definition is the one you must be concerned with: *to bring to the public attention.* More liberally, we may interpret this to mean *to place before the public.*

In the earliest times, placing creative work before the public was a simple matter. Songs were sung and tales were told around the campfire. Artists painted their pictures on the walls of caves or on handy stones. Writers carved their words into clay shards or painted them on the scraped skins of animals.

For millennia, these were the standards of publication, changing only to allow for the slow advance of technology. The walls of caves gave way to the walls of tombs, the songs around the campfire became the dramas in Greek theaters, and the potsherds and animal skins turned into papyrus and parchment. But publication remained almost a face-to-face affair, especially in Europe, where paper was not available and monks painstakingly copied manuscripts by hand, creating two or three copies a year. In fact, as recently as the early seventeenth century, even after the advent of the printing press in Europe, two hundred copies were considered a large print run for a book.

PUBLISHING THROUGH THE AGES

- Cave painting
- Tomb painting
- Poet-singers
- Clay or stone tablets
- Animal skins
- Wood slabs
- Papyrus sheets
- Scrolls
- Bound folios
- Hand-illuminated manuscripts
- Movable type
- Modern paper
- Bound printed books
- Newspapers and magazines
- Digital formats
- Electronic publishing
- E-books

As it did with almost everything else, the industrial revolution brought rapid and large advances to the printing and publishing industries. Mechanical typesetting machines made the production of large numbers of books significantly cheaper and easier and turned publishing from a business of art into a business of mass production.

This trend accelerated as innovations in the technology of type-setting and printing continued to advance, culminating in the high-speed automatic typesetting machines of the mid-twentieth century, with which it was possible to print millions of copies of any work from newspapers to magazines to books.

The Expansion of Print Publishing

The publishing industry, driven by heretofore undreamed of capabilities in the manufacture of its products, changed and expanded to meet the new technological developments. Mass production demanded new models of mass marketing and mass distribution in order to take full advantage of the increased capacity of the publishing industry to create product.

Another development was the worldwide population explosion during this period. During the twentieth century, aided by advances in public health, medicine and sanitation, world population doubled, then doubled again. This population increase was accompanied by a huge increase in literacy as public educational systems became the norm in western nations and made heavy inroads in other parts of the world.

The upshot of all this was that the market for the written word grew in tandem with the publishing industry's technological ability to meet the growing need. In just a few centuries, publishing was transformed from a small craft into a great industry.

Huge industries, by their nature, require a lot of money or capital investment. The market for writing had grown a thousandfold, but the money needed to reach this market had grown at least that much. One could still serve a small market without using capital-intensive methods; even by the middle of the twentieth century, a typewriter and a mimeograph machine were still sufficient to publish a newspaper or magazine with a few dozen or a few hundred subscribers. But if a writer hoped to reach a mass audience, *to place before the public* his work, it was necessary to deal with the great publishing empires with their tons of hot type and thousands of employees. But e-publishing is starting to change the necessity of working with a giant publishing house.

Publishing's Unusual Business Practices

E-publishing also has the power to affect the unusual, and often wasteful, business practices of traditional publishing. The modern publishing industry took shape according to the peculiar exigencies involved in the sale of its product: the printed word. It has been said, "If Henry Ford had sold cars the way publishers sell books, we'd still be riding horses."

There is some truth to the joke. If Ford sold cars the way publishers sell books, here is how it would go: Ford would make a million cars, store half of them in a warehouse and ship the rest to their dealers. The dealers wouldn't pay Ford for the cars until they were sold. At any time the dealers could decide that they didn't want to offer those models any longer. They would then return the full-size cars still on their lots to the automaker and receive credit on their outstanding bills. To receive the same credit on their compact cars, all they would need to do is tear the doors off the cars and send the doors back, tossing the rest of the vehicle into the local junkyard. (When bookstores "return" a paperback, they don't send the whole book—only the front and back covers. The rest is thrown away.)

This is a reasonable description of how publishers, even today, sell books. And this is how *your* book will be sold, if a mainstream print publisher sells it for you *today*.

Tomorrow will be another story. With e-publishing, the waste brought about by traditional publishing is completely avoidable. And for those of you reading this book to learn how to publish your book electronically, tomorrow has already arrived.

CHAPTER EIGHT

THE BENEFITS OF E-PUBLISHING OVER TRADITIONAL METHODS

You may still be unsure about whether e-publishing is a better option for you over traditional publishing. In actuality, there are many benefits to e-publishing besides the ability to reach more readers with greater ease. In this chapter, we'll explore some of these benefits.

E-Publishing Is Less Expensive and More Efficient Than Traditional Publishing

As we've pointed out, there are two primary definitions of publishing. The first is: "to prepare and issue material for public distribution or sale." The second is: "to bring to public attention."

These are long-established definitions that for centuries applied to print publication. They apply even more strongly to e-publishing, but you need to understand not only how the traditional meanings still apply, but how digital e-publishing has changed and expanded these traditional definitions.

Distribution: Traditional Vs. Digital

In the world of print publishing, distribution has always meant an extremely complicated system designed to move physical objects (printed books) from the publisher's printing operation into the hands of the individual consumer.

This system involves packing and shipping, interim distributors, end-market distributors including bookstores, discount clubs like Price-Costco, grocery store book racks, mail-order book clubs and libraries.

It also includes several different layers of accounting systems, as well as discount pricing models and various return policies at every level. To complicate matters further, books can be returned to the publisher for credit if not sold by the end retailer, which adds yet another layer of shipping and accounting cost, plus the physical discarding or destruction of books.

This traditional system is incredibly expensive, wasteful and destructive (some might even say "insane"), but until very recently, it is the only one we've had.

The single biggest change between the traditional publishing and e-publishing is that we are no longer talking about physical objects (with a few minor exceptions like CDs and print-on-demand books).

On page 40, we compare print publishing versus e-publishing in order to understand just how large and pervasive these changes are.

Professional writers are quite familiar with the traditional publishing process. They don't get paid royalties on books that are returned, which is fair enough. Those returned books aren't sales, because in the end, the publisher doesn't receive any money for them. In the world of author royalties, this process is called "sell-through." Sell-through is figured as books shipped (sold) minus books returned (unsold). In these times, it is not at all unusual for less than half of the books a publisher prints to actually end up being sold.

The Benefits of E-Publishing Over Traditional Methods

E-PUBLISHING VS.	**PRINT PUBLISHING**
• No physical objects as we traditionally understand them. E-books exist as digital files that have no tangible existence in the real world.	• Designed to move physical objects (printed books) from the publisher's printing operation to remote distribution and sales points.
• E-books exist as digital files and don't need to be put into boxes or shipped in order to reach their destinations. The closest thing to shipping charges would be the cost of accessing servers.	• Print books are physically put into boxes and shipped to various destinations. This is a cost-intensive process. Packing and shipping is also necessary when distributors *return* unsold books to the publisher.
• E-books are for the most part distributed directly from the publisher (even a one-person publisher) to the reader. In certain cases, a distribution middleman does exist, usually in the form of an online bookstore like Amazon.com.	• Print books are distributed according to several different models, all of which involve middlemen who exist in the space between the publisher and the reader. For instance, many small independent distributors don't buy directly from the publisher, but instead purchase from national distribution operations, who buy and store books from a publisher for resale to bookstores. Other types of regional distributors perform the same function for nonbookstore retailers like grocery stores, drugstores and airport terminals.

- In the world of e-publishing, accounting is much simpler. Integrated systems automatically track a book through the life of the much less complicated process of distribution. In the case of smaller e-publishers who market directly to the reader, five or six accounting systems can often be replaced by only one.

- Interim distributors, whether regional or national, duplicate these accounting systems. Finally, book retailers have their own profit and loss systems to maintain. One book can be counted five or six times as it makes its way through all these systems—all of which involve employees, computers and software to maintain.

- In the print world, each step in the distribution process involves another layer of accounting. The publishers keep track of how many books they have printed, stored as inventory, shipped, sold or had returned. They also must maintain a system of sales tracking to support their system of payments to authors.

- One of the largest costs built into the current methods of distributing print books is the returns system. As we said in the last chapter, "If Henry Ford sold cars the way we sell books, we'd still be riding horses." And, to the frustration of many writers, there's some truth to this statement. Almost all books a publisher ships to a distributor or retailer are accompanied by a money-back guarantee—and there is no time limit. If you buy a book from a bookstore, read it, then return it, they will simply return the book to the publisher for full credit. Wouldn't it be nice to buy your next Ford with that kind of deal?

With e-publishing, however, there are no returns because a book is "printed" only when a customer orders one. Sell-through can now approach, even achieve, 100 percent, thus eliminating the single most wasteful part of the current print publishing model.

Traditional publishers are highly aware of the potential cost savings in e-publishing's digital distribution model. More than any other factor, the promise of increased profits from less wasteful practices is driving traditional publishing houses toward some version of digital distribution. And you, too, can receive similar advantages as an individual e-publisher.

CHAPTER NINE

UNDERSTANDING THE DIGITAL REVOLUTION IN FIVE EASY STEPS

One: The Digital Revolution in a Nutshell

In its purest sense, electronic publishing is in full swing today. Every time you visit a Web page to read an author's chatty newsletter or download a short story or even a book, you are taking advantage of electronic publication. Every time you put your own work on a Web page or allow it to be downloaded by somebody else, you are acting as an electronic publisher. Every time you put a CD or a DVD game, book, video or music disk into your computer, you are consuming an electronically published product. Every time you burn a CD-ROM, you are "publishing" electronically.

The essence of electronic publishing is *the presentation of content in digital form*. It doesn't matter what that content is; sound, video, pictures or writing can all be reduced to bits and bytes and then packaged, published, transmitted, viewed and passed on to the millions of machines (and not just personal computers) able to interpret those bits and bytes.

Writers must understand this definition of electronic publishing because it is so far reaching and it affects everything about their literary creations, including distribution, marketing, sales and even the most basic concepts of intellectual property itself.

Two: Revolutionary Formats

Until the advent of digital electronic formats, the presentation of intellectual property—a legal term for an artist's creative work—was either entirely ephemeral (the songs heard round the campfire) or based on some real-world medium like print-on-paper, disks or tapes (or papyrus scrolls, chiseled stones or illuminated sheepskins). In order to permanently transfer the content, it was necessary to transfer some physical item—a book, a record, a videotape. This model, which has held sway for most of human history, had both advantages and disadvantages for the author. It allowed for a high degree of security: That is, one had to purchase a physical book in order to read it (or at least borrow it from a friend or library who purchased it). However, in order to widely distribute books, the author had to give away most of his potential profit to huge companies who had the capability to make, distribute and sell the book.

The ability to digitize intellectual content has destroyed that model. The reason is simple: Digital formats have entirely erased the notion of scarcity. Here's how that works.

Three: Scarcity—What It Means and Why It's Important

Until recently, in order to distribute a book widely, the book had to be printed. No matter how large the print run was, there was still a finite number of physical books created. If you wanted a copy, you had to buy one or borrow it from somebody else. Nor was it easy, if you wanted a second copy of the book, to make one yourself. Oh, you could tear the book apart and stick each page into a photocopier, but you would end up with a less appealing (though accurate) copy of the content. Further, the cost of your time to do this would be considerably greater than just buying another copy.

Until now, all of publishing has been based on the idea that books could only be produced in a finite, and therefore scarce, number of copies. Further, in order to make and market any large number of copies, a big industrial operation was required.

Digital formats do away with all that. What is a book anyway? Is it the physical book itself or the content presented therein? Think about it. When an author writes a book, he transcribes his thoughts into words that others can read and sets those words down on some medium that others can read—generally print on paper.

Is there any difference between a hardcover book and a paperback? How about an audio book on tape? They are certainly different physical items, but is the book itself different? Not at all. The book is the *content*, not the presentation of that content.

Digitization deals directly with the content itself, not the way it is presented. Once the content of a book has been rendered into bits and bytes as a computer file, it has the potential to be produced in almost any format: The file, for instance, can be fed into a computer-automated printing press and produced as a physical book printed on paper. Or it could be transferred into a sound file and distributed on a CD or an audiotape. It can reside on a computer hard drive and be viewed with a text editor or word processor. But most important, the file can be *copied*. And it can be copied infinitely.

Four: Infinite Copies

The ability to copy a book with such ease is the most revolutionary aspect of the digital age, and it threatens to change or destroy everything we've ever known about how books are created and published.

Here's an illustration: Let's say you've written a book. It sits on your computer hard drive as a digital file. You have a mailing list of ten friends to whom you want to send this book. You e-mail the file to each of those friends. What has really happened? Did you send the file that originally was on your hard drive? Nope. You sent each friend a *copy* of that file. You still have the original.

There is no real difference between mailing that file to ten friends or a million. Once the original content has been created in digital format, the number of copies that can be made is infinite. Further, each person who receives that file has the same ability to make as many copies as they wish and to do whatever they would like with them.

This ability to make unlimited copies of a digitized version of your book's content is at the heart of the digital revolution we now have entered, and it presents authors with both opportunities and problems that have never been seen before. Digital content has opened a Pandora's box of technology, and we have no idea what sort of good fairies or bad demons may yet come flying out.

E-publishing is one such spirit. Many regard it as a good fairy, but many others see it as the most evil of demons. For authors, a lot depends on your perspective: How do you, as a writer, see your work? What are your goals for it? What are your goals for yourself?

Do you, for instance, simply wish to place your work before as wide an audience as possible, with no thought to whether you get paid for it? Or do you only want readers who pay for the privilege to read your work? Maybe you would be willing to accept some combination of the two.

And what about issues of control? While it is exciting to think of millions of people reading your book, remember anything that can be copied can also be *changed*. How would you feel if one of those friends to whom you sent your novel opened it up in his word processor and wrote a new ending to the book, one he liked better than yours? Or added sections of ribald commentary? And then (remember, any digital format can be endlessly copied) sent your original work with his changes to his own list of a thousand friends?

Infinite copying means infinite loss of control. You may become unable to control what is done with your own intellectual property once you've distributed it in digital format to even one other person.

Five: Acts of Creation—Copyright Enforcement in a Digital Age

Which brings us to the question of content itself. You, as a writer, perform an *act of creation*, and the result of that act is content— the specific rendering of your ideas into a novel, a nonfiction book, or a collection of stories, essays or poems that can be read by others. But can they legally change your work? Under copyright laws, *ideas* cannot be copyrighted, only the specific *rendering* of ideas. You could take the idea, "boy meets girl, boy loses girl, boy regains girl in the end," and write innumerable specific variations of that general idea. Each story would be different. Each *story* based on that idea could be copyrighted, but the original idea itself cannot.

But what does digital format do to the idea of copyright? After all, copyright law is basically nothing more than law that governs the *right* to make *copies*. Up until very recently, laws like this were more or less enforceable. An author would "rent" the right to copy his original work to a publisher. The publisher would make lots of physical copies (books) and then distribute and sell them. If another publisher made a copy of the original book and then printed and sold any appreciable number of them, it was immediately obvious that the author's *right to copy* had been infringed.

But law is not written on stone, immutable and unchanging forever. Law responds to reality. As we noted earlier, the *ability* to make copies was never erased by law, only the legal right to do so. As a practical matter, making physical copies on a small scale was always possible, but it was constrained, not only by legal issues but also by relative difficulty. As mentioned earlier, it was simpler and cheaper to buy a new copy than to make one for yourself. The law and the real world worked together, one reinforcing the other.

What does the fact that it is now possible to make a million copies of a work with the click of a mouse button do to the whole notion of copyright law? There is no longer any practical restraint on making copies. Since making a copy of a digital format is now both effortless and free, how can copyright be enforced?

The answer is, it cannot. At least not yet, not in any way we have yet devised, though this is not to say that technology may not come up with something practical in the future. Unfortunately, that future has not yet arrived.

The implications are enormous. We will discuss many of them at greater depth later in this book. They affect not just writers, but all creators of intellectual property, from musicians, to filmmakers, to software programmers. And those implications inform every aspect of this wonderful—and frightening—new world of electronic publishing.

Bet you didn't think much about *this* when you posted your diary—or first chapters of your novel—on your Web site, did you?

CHAPTER TEN

DOES *YOUR* INFORMATION WANT TO BE FREE?

The origins of the phrase "Information wants to be free" are misty. Some variations of it predate the Internet. One could make a case that it is merely a twist on the New Testament's John 8:32, "You shall know the truth, and the truth shall make you free."

It is a matter of record, however, that Peter Samson, a member of the Tech Model Railroad Club at MIT, said "Information should be free," somewhere around 1959, and that Stewart Brand, creator of the *Whole Earth Catalog*, founder of The WELL, writer, thinker and all-around public intellectual, said in a speech at the first Hacker's Conference in 1984, "On the one hand information wants to be expensive, because it's so valuable. The right information in the right place just changes your life. On the other hand, information wants to be free, because the cost of getting it out is getting lower and lower all the time. So you have these two fighting against each other."

The phrase has become a rallying cry of the digital age for many and an anathema for as many more. Most who use it focus on the second part of Brand's statement and ignore the first—that part about information wanting to be expensive because it's so valuable. And there is something Brand didn't mention: Information has *costs*. No matter what sort of information it is, it costs *something* to produce in a usable form.

Information Has Costs

Everybody has heard the even more ubiquitous phrase, "Time is money." What this means is that time itself has value. Every writer understands this on some level. When you sit down at your keyboard (or typewriter, or with your favorite pen or pencil, for you Luddites out there), you have at least some awareness that the time you spend writing could also be used for something else. You could be walking the dog, or cleaning the refrigerator, or making love—or earning your money doing something else. So, in essence, you place greater value on the time you spend writing than you do on spending (there's that money notion again!) time on these other things.

Admittedly, the idea seems somewhat nebulous. Most writers perceive a difference in value between giving up washing the car and receiving a check from a publisher for ten thousand dollars as reimbursement for their creative efforts. In principle, though, the idea of value remains consistent. Creation has costs. Which leads directly to the corollary: *Somebody has to pay those costs.*

"Information wants to be free." It's an attractive notion to some, but at bottom, it is a lie. "Information" doesn't want to do anything. Information in the digital age is little atom-sized squiggles in magnetic fields. What's actually going on is that some, probably many, *people* want information to be free.

And why wouldn't they? They've been trained to believe that much of the information they get every day is already free.

Richard T. Kaser, the executive director of the National Federation of Abstracting & Information Services, had this to say in an excellent article published in the May 2000 issue of *D-Lib Magazine* (www.dlib.org/dlib/may00/kaser/05kaser.html):

If Information Wants to Be Free . . . Then Who's Going to Pay for It?

The following is an odd point to make when addressing publishers, but we simply cannot overlook the fact that the notion that information ought to be free is ingrained in our culture. I would even go so far as to say that you as individuals also believe this. And I'm going to prove it to you.

When you go to the library, you expect to check out a book for free. When you turn on your radio, you expect to listen to music for free. When you turn on your TV, you expect to watch network programming for free. You, like everyone else, have come to believe that information is free.

Still, there's a double standard. If you want to personally own a copy of that book you checked out of the library, you are willing to pay for a copy. If you want to personally own a copy of that song you heard on the radio, you are willing to pay for the CD. If you want to personally own a copy of the movie you just watched, you are willing to buy the video.

I conclude from this that, as a society, we pay for the medium and not the message. As a society we perceive that the value resides in the copy, not in the content . . . which is free . . . free to use again and again and again, free to reuse (say, if we want to quote something or lift a fact) . . . and free to give away to a friend or resell once you are done with it. All of this is ingrained in our thinking. It's not new.

The critical point that Kaser makes here is this: We have become accustomed to paying for the *medium* but not the *message*. Yet the *message* is precisely what we, as writers, are in the business of creating and have been since that very first singer gathered an audience around a smoky fire and gave voice to the literature of the day.

E-publishing strips this fact naked and forces us to recognize it for the first time in history, because e-publishing, like many of the other offshoots and implications of the digital revolution, destroys the entire concept of "medium." By making content, information, equally and cheaply copyable to all media—paper, tape, disk, chip, hard drive—it makes any specific medium irrelevant. But if the medium no longer costs anything and we already believe the content to be free, then where does that leave those of us who spend the time, effort and talent to create that content and would like to be repaid in some measure for our work?

It leaves us with a problem or two, is what we would say.

All Is Not Lost

E-publishing is still in its infancy (its drooling infancy, some say) with the answers to most of these quasi-philosophical questions yet to be resolved. In some cases, the questions have yet to even be asked, and we wouldn't bring them up except for the uncomfortable fact that "quasi-philosophy" has a disconcerting way of showing up in the distinctly unphilosophical everyday world and putting a terrible hitch in your daily gitalong.

For example, how will you ensure you receive payment for your writing? Some parts of this book address the concerns of those for whom questions of cost and payment are not large issues; but the bulk of it is aimed at the writer who hopes, in some fashion, to be paid for the effort of creation.

As we have noted, the world of electronic publishing is still in flux and is likely to remain so for quite some time. When this proposal was first placed before our publishers, the makers of the Rocket eBook and the SoftBook existed as going concerns. Now, both those products have vanished into a larger corporation that makes different models of e-book readers. The state of things only a year down the road can't be predicted with utter certainty. But through the technological fog, some things are becoming more clear, and other things remain unchanged.

Somebody still has to transfer the idea into usable information. Somebody still has to *write the book*. That somebody is you. Read on to learn how to go about it as we all try to ride the crest of the greatest wave of change in human history.

CHAPTER ELEVEN

PROTECTING WHAT'S YOURS: DIGITAL RIGHTS MANAGEMENT

Digital rights management, which we will henceforth refer to as "DRM," is one of those things authors wish they didn't have to think about, just as most authors don't want to worry about *contracts*, or *marketing*, or *distribution*, or any other nuts and bolts that go into publishing. Time was when you didn't have to worry—much—about these aspects of publication, either. You wrote your magnum opus, put a stack of manuscript pages into a box and sent it out. If you were good enough or lucky enough, an agent read your work and agreed to represent you. The agent then tried to sell your book to a publishing house. Between them, your agent and publisher took care of all those pesky details. But digital publishing has the potential to be much more transparent than anything that has come before. This can be an advantage, but it also means that you, the writer, have to work a lot harder doing the things that the traditional agent-publisher relationship used to do for you.

Digital rights management is a fancy way of describing a process that tries to determine who gets to make copies of your work. Remember, the concept at the heart of copyright law is the *right to copy*. Copyright law (with certain exceptions) states that you, as the creator of the work, have the right to say who can make copies of it. After all, what is old-style publishing anyway? Nothing more than somebody with a printing press running off thousands of copies of the manuscript you created. A publisher has to make copies before it can sell them, and you control the right to allow those copies to be made.

Think of "digital rights" as being "copyright for digital content." The "management" part of the phrase refers to a collection of various schemes, some digital, some electronic, created to allow the rights-holder, whoever it might be, to maintain control over who gets to make copies of the digital content.

But as we've previously noted, one of the reasons that copyright law in general was reasonably enforceable was that making copies of things was hard. Let's compare this idea with movies: Prior to the VCR, making a copy of a movie was, for all intents and purposes, impossible for the average viewer. With a VCR, of course, it isn't difficult to make a single copy of a movie as you watch it on television. At one point both the TV and film industries fought the notion of allowing you to do this, but eventually, faced by the prospect of not being able to enforce any sort of prohibition that would prevent individual copying, they grudgingly conceded the point.

With music, we have the Napster phenomenon to consider. Until the advent of tape recorders, it was unfeasible for a private individual to make a copy of a musical performance. After tapes became ubiquitous, it was possible for a person to make a few copies without great difficulty. Once again, what would appear to be a violation of copyright became more or less acceptable because new deals were worked out that added a bit to the cost of every tape deck so that manufacturers could pay a sort of generic "royalty" to the producers of music.

What Napster demonstrated was the power of digital duplication. Remember, once something is in digital format—that is, a computer file—it can be copied an unlimited number of times with almost no effort. Within two years, Napster went from non-existence to a distributed "service" claiming more than sixty million members, all of whom were interested in "sharing"—and what that really means is copying—music files from one person's computer to another's over the Internet. In that short period, billions of copies of copyright-protected music were made and distributed across the entire globe.

There is no material difference between a computer file of *Metallica's Greatest Hits* and one of Shakespeare's greatest plays—or one that contains your labor of blood, sweat and tears. Any and all can be shared without limit. With the advent of the digital age, copyright—your right to permit or not permit people to copy your work—is more threatened than ever before in history.

Just about everybody in the publishing industry understands this; and while there is some disagreement as to the appropriate response, DRM is an area currently of great interest, particularly among the mainstream publishing houses who see their traditional business model at tremendous risk.

There is a great deal of debate about just how effective these schemes are, or will be, and we will discuss the matter in greater depth at a later point. Most of the methods, both currently in use or proposed for the future, are quite complicated. The basic idea, however, is simple: Think of DRM as it applies to e-publishing as "technological ways to control who is allowed to copy your e-book."

CHAPTER TWELVE

THE NUTS AND BOLTS
OF WRITING AN E-BOOK

The legendary science fiction author, Robert Heinlein, in a 1947 essay on writing speculative fiction, said:

1. You must write.
2. You must finish what you write.
3. You must refrain from rewriting, except to editorial order.
4. You must put the work on the market.
5. You must keep the work on the market until it is sold.

There have been some changes since Heinlein's time. First, you'd be well advised to give some thought as to who you see (or would like to see) as the potential audience for your writing. Do you see your reader sitting in front of a full-size desktop computer, reading your work off a large screen? Or perhaps it's some harried businessman trapped in a congested airport waiting area, looking to while away a little time with some light reading he's tucked away on his laptop. Or somebody with a Palm digital assistant reading your latest creation on a screen not much larger than a pack of cigarettes.

Let's face it: None of the current incarnations of digital reading technology yet fully match the ease and experience of a good old-fashioned printed book. Some come close, and in the future, the technology will continue to improve until it meets or exceeds the way we've read for thousands of years. On the other hand, does reading Tolstoy's *War and Peace* on a Palm Pilot sound like something you'd enjoy doing?

What Sort of E-Writing Works Right Now?

In general, short texts are currently better received than long ones. Even Stephen King broke up his online novel *The Plant* into shorter sections. However, you need not feel limited: If a novel or long nonfiction work is bubbling up inside you, let it flow. After all, in the end the decision of whether—and how—to read your work will be up to the reader. And with electronic publication, you have the potential to allow an enormous number of readers to make these decisions.

Another option is the serialized work. You may write something of considerable length, but you e-publish it in short sections so that the reader doesn't have to cope with huge files and downloads but is still titillated into coming back for more—if only to find out what happens next!

Will you be writing fiction or nonfiction? Again, it makes no difference in the long run, but you should be aware that there are elements of e-publishing that seem almost tailored to nonfiction.

For example, the ability to search a file for a specific topic makes a nonfiction e-book very useful to its readers. Prior to digital formats, you were limited to using chapter headings and indexes to find that elusive bit of information you wanted in some huge textbook or operations manual. Now, you can simply plug a word or phrase into the search function of the machine containing the e-book and instantly find what you're looking for.

Another function that is increasingly available in many computerized reading platforms is the ability to use an interactive dictionary. Just click on the word in the text you don't understand and up pops a dictionary telling you the exact definition and even, in some cases, pronouncing the word aloud for you. This is an invaluable aid for those of you who, like this author, have what is called a "reading vocabulary," that is, words picked up from the writing of others that we've carefully looked up, but still don't really know how to pronounce correctly—until we mispronounce them in front of somebody who does know, and who gently corrects us (or worse, *doesn't* correct us, so that we can make fools of ourselves all over again).

These interactivity features of e-reading work perfectly well with either fiction or nonfiction, of course, but in some ways they seem most ideal for works of a technical or reference nature. Once again, though, the choice will be yours.

CHAPTER THIRTEEN

AVOIDING COMMON WRITING PITFALLS

It's beyond the scope of this book to try to teach you how to write. But don't despair: There are thousands of books out there that will do just that, as well as writing courses both online and in schools and colleges everywhere. The publishers of this book offer dozens of excellent books on the art and craft of writing. No doubt you will find one that deals directly with the subject in which you are interested. Take a look at www.writers digest.com for a complete list of what is available.

Check with your local community college or, if available, a university or university extension campus. Almost all offer creative writing courses that you can take without becoming part of a full degree program. Some of these courses are offered online.

There are also a host of inexpensive or free writing courses offered via the Web. The best way to find these is to plug "online writing course" (without the quote marks) into a good search engine like Google (www.google.com) or AltaVista (www.altavista.com). Use common sense. Quite often, you get what you pay for, although this is not to say that free courses may not be excellent. Look for courses with instructors who have professional writing credits, especially credits in the writing area you wish to pursue.

Other options are writing workshops or critique groups. While these may not provide the breadth of instruction a more formal writing course would, they can often offer a great deal of value in the input from other writers. No matter how hard we all try to be objective about our own work, most writers will find outside viewpoints helpful. Many such workshops function entirely online, but depending on your location, you can also find these groups meeting in the "real world." Check bulletin boards at local bookstores, grocery stores and coffee houses, classified ads in newspapers, even your local librarians—who are, by the way, wonderful sources of information on almost any subject.

Once you've finished writing a draft, you aren't done—even if your only intention is to post your work on your own Web site, where the only person you have to convince to let you publish it is yourself.

Remember who your competition is: It's not just other self-publishing Web authors. It is every writer producing work for every possible publishing media, from print books to proprietary e-book formats to the Web itself. In order to be competitive, your own work must measure up in the quality of its presentation to the best there is. Thanks to e-publishing, your work must compete with a vast selection of reading choices that include you—and Stephen King, Danielle Steele and Shakespeare.

What would you think if you bought a book at your local bookshop, opened it up, began to read and found several grammatical errors, a couple of misspellings and an assorted typo or two on the first page? How much farther would you read, even if this book was presented as being a great work of literature?

You probably wouldn't read very far, first, because all those mistakes would be distracting. They pull the reader out of the "immersion" in the story that makes up an enjoyable reading experience. Errors remind you forcefully that you're reading a book, not experiencing the tale. Second, common sense alone would tell you that

> **JUST BETWEEN US**
>
> Look, let's be honest here: Writing talent will play a major role in how well your writing is accepted. But a very talented writer can easily sabotage her own work by improperly presenting it. You *must* eliminate the technical errors. You cannot allow misspellings, common grammar errors or typos to litter your presentation.

any author who presented work (or allowed it to be presented) in such a sloppy manner probably approached the craft aspect of writing in a similarly disappointing way.

Wage War on Literary Sloppiness

Unfortunately, avoiding mistakes is easier said than done. What can you do on your own? One of the most useful features of major word processors (which in my estimation makes them worth using over simple text editors) is the ability to check spelling, either as you type or afterwards. If you do use such a word processor, make sure you use this feature! We prefer the "belt-and-suspender" approach; we spell-check both while typing and afterwards.

Grammar problems are a bit trickier, especially since writers often break grammatical rules intentionally. However, this is no excuse for confusing "its" with "it's" or making a similar faux pas. Full-featured word processors also include grammar checkers, which function in much the same way that spell checkers do. Unfortunately, these grammar checkers seem slanted toward the very basic grammar used in business correspondence. Many writers (myself included) find them too much of a distraction while writing prose and turn them off. This is your choice. A good word processor will at least allow the writer to use its grammar checker to catch those pesky "itsies."

Once you've done your basic job and made sure your manuscript is as free of misspellings, grammatical errors and miscellaneous typos as possible, you move beyond the realm of proofreading and into proper editing.

Thanks to the Web, the number of editing resources available to you are much more numerous than they previously were. Nevertheless, there are pitfalls that accompany this advantage. Read on to learn the whole story.

CHAPTER FOURTEEN

HOW TO FIND A TRUSTWORTHY EDITOR FOR YOUR E-BOOK

O ne of the great advantages of the mainstream model of publishing is that your manuscript will be reviewed by an alert editor—and sometimes by multiple editors. Conversely, one of the principal advantages of e-publishing is that you aren't always limited by the hurdles of acceptance and rejection involved in achieving mainstream print publication.

In order to compete with all the other e-books we discussed in the previous chapters, your work should be brought to its highest possible level. You must have somebody with the necessary editing skills objectively read and critique your work. If you have a friend who is a professional writer or editor, this might be a possibility. Unfortunately, such folks are often very busy with their own projects, and, even with the best of intentions, will tend to regard doing a "freebie" for you as, at best, a job well down their to-do list and, at worst, an afterthought to be done when they get around to it, which often turns out to be never.

If you belong to a writing or criticism group that includes professionals, you may be able to obtain good results, at least with the "big chunks." By this, I mean that the group criticism process will at least turn up the major holes in your work. For some writers, this is enough.

But if you want a paragraph by paragraph reading, with full and objective criticism of all aspects of your tale, you will probably need to hire a professional. I can hear you groaning now: "Oh, no, how do I do *that*? And how much will it cost?"

Prices can vary significantly. Read the short article by Susan Malone (below) to help understand what you should expect to receive for your dollar.

Susan M. Malone (www.maloneeditorial.com), contributing editor to Authorlink.com, associate editor for *The Literary Magazine*, multipublished author, and owner of Malone Editorial Services (www.maloneeditorial .com), has this to say about hiring a freelance editor:

"Editorial services/book doctors abound. And the disparity in pricing boggles the mind. What gives here? Why does one charge $1 per page and another $8 (I've even heard rumors of up to $15)? And what about all of those in between?

"Basically, the services provided divide into separate though often overlapping categories. So, let's just briefly discuss them.

"The lower ranges will generally net you a copy edit—punctuation, grammar, spelling, etc.—and an overall assessment (4–5 pages) of your work as a whole. A 'surface' read, this proves most helpful to accomplished writers, ones who already understand the blueprints for fashioning salable fiction and nonfiction by having taken classes, attended ongoing writers' workshops, and participated in conferences and seminars. I.e., those who have put in the time and effort to hone their craft. Even then, a more hands-on approach is sometimes called for, especially when, after doing all of the above, you're still getting form rejections.

"Also included in this lesser-fee range are agent reading fees. But beware here. The Association of Authors' Representatives (AAR) doesn't allow the agents under its membership to charge for this service. And besides, you want your agent out there selling, not spending time fine-tuning manuscripts. These days, those are two very different jobs.

"The middle to upper ranges deal with an entirely different beast altogether. Here we get into the true nuts and bolts of writing, and you can expect a great deal more from the dollars spent.

"Rather than the comment, 'The character is flat,' an in-depth edit should address why the character comes off as such, explain exactly how to flesh him or her out, and show specifically where to do so. Instead of, "The pacing is off," this edit targets where the story-line, plot, characters, dialogue, etc., bog down, and then delineates exactly where and specifically how to fix it.

"Most importantly, an in-depth edit explains the whys—those elusive, subtle tools of writing that prove difficult to teach in the group classroom, and can take years of study to learn. Experienced authors and editors know these tools, and the good ones can teach them to you.

"The very upper end of the scale is occupied by ghostwriters—those who actually take your work and rewrite it, sometimes requiring co-author credits, sometimes not, but always with a hefty price tag (up to $30,000).

"Once you decide to pursue the editorial route, by all means research the firms available, find out which services they provide, and at what cost. Ask pertinent questions, gather data, and then make your decisions accordingly. Of course, the old adage comes into play here as well: 'You get what you pay for.'

"But by all means, demand that your editor allow for discussion and follow-up once his or her work is complete. This should not only be an edit, but a true learning experience as well. And learning is a two-way street, a dialogue, not a sterile endeavor undertaken in a vacuum."

March 1999, authorlink.com, www.authorlink.com/ask_ed_99c.htm

How to Find a Trustworthy Editor for Your E-Book

Researching Editorial Services

Once you've decided how much money you are willing to spend, how do you go about researching editorial services? How do you make sure you avoid those who won't give you your dollars' worth? One good way is to talk to authors who have used specific editors and found them to be satisfactory. And if you don't know any authors, fear not! The Internet can ride to your rescue. There are Usenet news groups like misc.writing, alt.writing and many others where you can ask questions and get answers from writers of every different level all over the world. The Yahoo! Web site maintains hundreds of different discussion groups, many of which concern writers and writing. Check them out at http://groups.yahoo.com/.

Keep in mind that many of these groups (technically called listservs, mailing lists or newsgroups) have been in existence for a long time and have established set ways of communication. It is best for the newcomer to "lurk" (read but do not reply or post) for a while, until he has a good feel for what is acceptable etiquette. Some of the groups, especially the Usenet newsgroups, regularly post "FAQs" (lists of Frequently Asked Questions—and their answers), which you'd do well to read before posting to ask a question that has already been answered hundreds of times. Another advantage to first reading the FAQs, if available, is that they are often gold mines of general information about the topics of discussion in the group. You may even find the information on freelance editors right there on the Web site.

○ ○ ○

Whew! Now your book is written and edited. It was a lot of work just to get to the beginning of the e-publishing process! Nevertheless, it is absolutely critical that you do that work. Remember, e-publishing is only a way of presenting your work to the public. What happens then is dependent on the work itself—on your writing and the talent, skill, craft and technical care you bring to it. So make sure that what you intend to e-publish is the very best you are capable of. Your readers will thank you for it.

PART TWO

Getting Started: Writing and Formatting Your E-Book

CHAPTER FIFTEEN

GETTING YOUR BOOK INTO A DIGITAL FORMAT

H ow do you get your book into digital format?

The simplest answer is to create it in a digital format in the first place. By definition, anything written on a computer is created in digital format because that format is all modern computers understand. When you use a computer to write something, you create a *file* containing your words and then *save* that file onto a computer's hard drive or some other storage medium like a floppy disk, a ZIP disk or even magnetic tape. That file is automatically in digital format; not words, but an arrangement of bits and bytes, of ones and zeros, that a computer program can recognize and transform into a format (words) that other humans can easily read and understand.

Many writers prefer to use *word processors* to do this task. By far the dominant word processor in use today is the various versions of Microsoft Word.

If you've been limited to pointed sticks or clumsy mechanical "home printers" (typewriters), the first time you use a computerized word processor may seem like a dream come true.

No more trying to decipher some scrawled word you wrote two paragraphs ago that you can now no longer figure out. Your word processor renders your creations into whatever clearly readable font

CREATE DIGITAL TEXT WITH:

- Simple text editors.
- Full-featured word processors or desktop publishing programs.
- By scanning typewritten pages yourself or paying a service to do it for you.
- By having manuscript pages transcribed by professional services.
- By dictating manuscript pages directly to your computer.

you desire. Editing is a snap. You can add to or delete from your writing merely by typing or by clicking your mouse. You don't have to grab a lever on your typewriter and push the platen back in order to start a new line. A word processor automatically moves on to the next line. Maybe best of all, especially for those of us who didn't do so well back in Miss Grundy's second-grade spelling class, word processors offer the ability to *spell-check*, not only after the work is written, but even as you write it. Most full-featured word processors even offer, for those who desire it, a *grammar checker*, which will gently nudge you if the program thinks you may have committed some grammatical horror—think of Miss Grundy in an electronic can, forever nagging you about the difference between "its" and "it's" . . .

Full-featured processors like Microsoft Word, Corel WordPerfect (www3.corel.com/cgi-bin/gx.cgi/AppLogic+FTContentServer ?pagename=Corel/Product/Details&id=CC11NDB84AC) and StarOffice StarWriter (www.sun.com/software/star/staroffice/5.2/ whatsnew/writer.html) all offer comparable writing tools, and all are also capable of creating files that other word processors can use, as well as directly using files created by other word processors.

This ability to "import and export" files comes in handy for the author who prefers to use something other than Microsoft Word, because Word has become the standard in the publishing industry.

Most mainstream publishing houses will request that the author submit computer files of his work in the Word format; and since publishers, if not always right, usually always win, it's comforting to be able to give them what they want, no matter what format you originally used.

As we've noted previously, full-featured word processors are able to do much more than what we've outlined above. While they are capable of creating text manuscripts with perfectly legible black fonts on white paper (Courier 12 is considered the standard font), properly formatting your words (a one-inch margin, double-spaced lines and a half-inch indentation to begin each paragraph), producing consecutively numbered pages, and so on, this only touches on the most basic functions of these programs. High-end word processors can do much more because in reality they are *desktop publishing systems.*

Expert users can render their work in a nearly infinite variety of presentations, from the basic "looks like it was written on a type-writer" layout we just described, to layouts indistinguishable from professionally published books, magazines and newspapers.

In the print publishing world, the production of books, magazines and newspapers still requires an army of specialists: copy editors who check for spelling and grammar errors; designers who create page layouts; an art department responsible for photographs, visual graphics, typeface and font design, and so on; and the press-room, which takes all the work of these experts and turns it into metal plates and mashes those plates against millions of pieces of paper to produce a finished product.

The digital revolution has given you, the author, the ability to do all of these tasks for yourself, from the initial creation to the final production. Many of you will find this to be overkill, but I have become accustomed to taking my own manuscripts and turning them into a few copies of simple, hand-bound books for purposes of soliciting criticism. I've discovered that people read books differently than they do manuscripts, and if you ask somebody to take a look at your latest book, there's nothing that compares to handing them a *book* to read. I mention this because it demonstrates what a great change has occurred; what once took hundreds of people and a huge industrial establishment to create, I—with my personal computer and a bit of knowledge about simple bookbinding techniques—can now easily do on my own.

I Hate Word Processors

You may say, "Word processing programs are too big, too expensive. I can't figure out all those options, and even if I could, I'll never use them." If this is your attitude, fear not. You aren't alone—many writers feel overwhelmed at first. But most programs are surprisingly easy.

All major computer operating systems provide some sort of program that allows you to edit simple text. In Microsoft Windows operating systems, the Notepad program lets you create simple, mostly unformatted text files. Wordpad, included with the more recent Windows operating systems, is a text processor with more features than Notepad, though it is much less complicated than Microsoft Word.

There are also hundreds of cheap or free text editors available on the World Wide Web for anyone to download. We have found the software archives at CNET's Download.com (http://download .cnet.com) as well as those at Tucows (www.tucows.com) to be extensive, easy to search and easy to obtain downloads from. There are many other archives, some specializing in a single operating system like Apple's Macintosh (the MacOSArchives at www.macos archives.com) or the evermore popular Linux operating system (DaveCentral's Linux archives at http://linux.davecentral.com). Shareware and freeware programs have become so widespread that you can be reasonably certain you will be able to find a text editor of some kind that will work with whatever combination of computer and operating system you have.

What If I Hate Computers?

The act of writing is one of the most unique and personal artistic activities imaginable. Every writer has his or her own rhythms, own creative comfort level, own persnickety preferences—or downright crotchety prejudices. Some folks cannot imagine typing their words and watching them appear on a computer screen. For them, perhaps it is the solid feel of a freshly sharpened number two pencil or the comforting heft of a well-used ink pen that lets the words pour out. Others may be unable to find inspiration without the snap and rattle of a just-unwrapped notebook filled with rich, creamy paper. Or maybe it's the click, clack and *ting*! of that old Underwood portable typewriter that sends your creative juices flooding into torrents of productivity. It really doesn't matter—whatever gets the work out of your skull, through that bleeding forehead Gene Fowler talked about, and into some kind of form somebody else can read is just fine. Remember, the creation of the work comes *first*. Everything else is just massaging the content.

Unfortunately, those notebooks filled with thousands of lines of carefully inscribed, perfectly legible copperplate (Hah! Don't we all wish?) or the several hundred pages of lovingly typed manuscript aren't in digital format. And they will have to be somehow transferred into that format in order to take advantage of the options available in the world of electronic publishing. In other words, you may have a book, but you don't have an e-book. Not yet, at least.

Are you doomed? Not at all. Unfortunately, even the most adamant computerphobe will have to resort to the hated machine in order to accomplish the transformation from words on paper to words as digits. (Remember those ones and zeros we talked about?)

Until recently, the most common method was to *scan* the words into a computer, then use some sort of *optical character recognition* (OCR) software program to recognize them and translate them into digital format. This presents a problem for the author who prefers to write by hand. OCR systems able to recognize personal handwriting are still in the research stage, and even those currently in development are not very good. So if you've got a stack of handwriting-filled notebooks, you will still have to put them into something a currently available OCR program can recognize—and that means an easily readable font like courier or arial.

But wait! If you have to do that anyway, why bother with OCR at all? Just type the words into a computer. Of course, if you hate computers too much to use them at all, then you'll have to find another option. The most obvious is to pay for some sort of secretarial or transcription service. There are thousands of them; even in the smallest of towns, there will usually be somebody able to translate your scrawls into a digital file on a floppy disk. High school and university students are often available at a reasonable price. Contact your local school's job resource center for information. Expect to pay from one to three dollars a page.

If you typed your manuscript and don't hate computers too much to use them at all, you are in luck. You'll need an additional piece of equipment called an *optical scanner*, which operates in much the same way as a photocopier does: You place a page of manuscript in the scanner, it "reads" it and makes a picture that can be viewed with a computer. These pictures of your typewritten pages can then be translated by an OCR program into digital text.

Scanners are quite cheap these days. Many perfectly adequate models are available for less than a hundred dollars, and, pleasantly enough, most scanners come with a software package that includes some sort of OCR program at no extra cost. OCR technology is by no means perfect, however, and any scanned text will then have to be carefully proofread before further use. Owning a scanner will come in handy later if you want to add art in your e-book.

As you might expect, just as there are transcription services that translate handwriting into digital text, there is also a host of scanning/OCR services that will perform the same task with typewritten pages. But you will always have the trade-off between the cost of these services, which is sometimes quite high, or the money-saving advantage of learning how to do it for yourself.

Make Your Computer Your Own Personal Secretary

Talking to your computer seems like science fiction, but this option is already practical and will become more so in the next few years.

There are already several *speech recognition programs* that let you dictate to your computer. The "big three" of these programs are: IBM's ViaVoice (www-4.ibm.com/software/speech/desktop/), Lernout & Hauspie's Voice Express (www.lhsl.com/voicexpress/) and Dragon's Naturally Speaking (www.dragonsys.com). These programs are fairly expensive, require a high-powered computer and a fair amount of technical knowledge to install and run. However, with practice, most of you will be able to dictate directly to your computer with 95 percent or better accuracy.

Perhaps more attractive, for those of you who like the sound of this option, is the addition of speech recognition capabilities to the very latest word processors like Microsoft Word XP at no extra cost. Word processor speech recognition is not yet at the level of the stand-alone programs, but you may find it workable for your own purposes. The price is certainly right.

As you can see from this chapter, there are many ways to skin the cat of digital formats. Which one you choose will be up to you. As long as the end product results in your work transformed into the digital format that computers can make use of, you have accomplished the primary requirement of entering the world of e-publishing—your creative content in digital format.

CHAPTER SIXTEEN

THE NEXT STEP: THREE E-PUBLISHING OPTIONS

OK, you've got a digital file. Now what?

First, congratulations! Welcome to the world of electronic publishing!

Now you have some decisions to make. The biggest one of all is what you want to do with your work. As far as e-publishing goes, you have three basic options for publishing your book:

- You can publish and distribute your work on your own site on the World Wide Web, either free or for some payment.
- You can license your work to an e-publisher, who will pay you for the right to create the book in various formats (either on a handheld reader or on the reader's computer), market it and give you a fee (royalty) for each book sold. This is similar to the traditional publishing model but transferred to a digital paradigm.
- You can pay an e-publisher to present and market your book to the public. This is called "vanity publishing."

Let's take a look at these in order. We'll discuss all of them in depth later, but a quick glance at the highlights of each will be useful as an aid to your decision-making process.

The Next Step: Three E-Publishing Options

Personal World Wide Web Publishing

This option is one that many would-be e-publishing authors are most interested in. It is also the most revolutionary, from a publishing standpoint, because it "short-circuits" the entire mainstream publishing model that has held sway for centuries.

In a nutshell: You post your work in digital format on a site accessible via the World Wide Web and thereby make it available to anybody who can surf the Web.

The requirements are relatively simple.

- You need to get your work into digital format.
- You need to have a connection to the Internet.
- You need to have a Web site.
- You need to "post" your work onto your Web site.

While this glosses over many details—sadly, nothing about technology is ever as easy as it looks at first glance—that's pretty much all there is to it. We'll get to those pesky details later.

Traditional Publishing in a Digital Paradigm

This method is potentially the simplest of all. There are now e-publishing companies that use the Internet as their primary distribution channel and e-books as their primary format. Such operations may also offer *print-on-demand* books, which are paper books printed one by one each time a customer orders them. They operate in almost exactly the same way that traditional print publishers do. However, since these e-publishers will pay *you* for the right to market, distribute and sell your work, you must create something that the publisher believes has a chance of making a profit. In other words, your initial customer isn't the individual reader, it is the publishing house itself—and as legions of would-be writers can attest, this is not an easy barrier to break.

Vanity Publishing

The vanity publishing model is almost identical to the mainstream publishing model, with one major exception: Authors *pay* the publishing house to publish their work. This lowers the publication barrier nearly to zero, but does present other problems to the writer, which we will discuss later in this book.

CHAPTER SEVENTEEN

UNDERSTANDING THE WORLD WIDE WEB AND THE INTERNET

We've mentioned Web pages (sometimes called Web sites or home pages) and the World Wide Web (the WWW) several times. Given the enormous amount of publicity the Web has received in other media, as well as the amazing growth in computer ownership and the number of computers connected to the Internet, one might think there's no mystery about what all the terms associated with the Web mean. But technical terms are often confusing, so here's a basic primer to help you understand these terms as we use them throughout this book.

- **The Internet:** The "Net" is nothing more than millions of computers connected with each other, mostly by telephone wires or larger cables. The Net is not the Web, though the Web depends on the Net in order to exist and function.

- **Web pages:** Think of the Net as a vast road system that carries traffic among millions of destination points: over the hills and through the woods, from your house to Grandma's house, perhaps. And think of Web pages as big signs mostly built around the traffic intersections of the road system. You drive along the road, and whenever you come to a cloverleaf, you see a bunch of signs. Those are Web pages, and each one has a single unique address.

So you could tell somebody: "Drive along Route 80 until you reach the Cloverdale turnoff. Right there, at 100 E. Cloverdale is a big billboard with stuff on it. That's my sign. I built it, and the people that own the Cloverdale turnoff let me put it up at their place. Why don't you head over there and take a look? I have my book written on it."

This is oversimplification, of course, but it gets the basic idea right. Now, let's extend the analogy a bit further.

- **Web browsers:** Let's say that your book is "written" on your billboard in a special "language" that can only be read if you look at the billboard through a special pair of eyeglasses, magical spectacles that automatically translate that language into one you understand. Most people who own computers these days have a special piece of software on their machines called a Web browser. Think of this "browser" as your "magic spectacles" that let you "view" that billboard. Now, these glasses have another property (We said they're magic, didn't we?). They are able to find every single billboard in the whole world, and let you look at them.

That's what a Web browser does. You give it the address of the Web page you want to look at, and it goes out, finds that page, makes a copy of it and presents that copy on your very own computer screen so you can read it in a language you understand.

Many of you will be interested in building one of those "billboards" along the information superhighway for yourself. You can put your writing on it, so that anyone in the world with a Web browser can read it. Luckily, it is easier than ever before to build your own billboard and get it planted next to the Infobahn (that's German for "information road"—the Web, by the way, is multilingual . . .).

Pretty neat idea, isn't it?

Welcome to the World Wide Web, the most revolutionary "highway" in history.

Understanding the World Wide Web and the Internet

Something to Keep in Mind

Definitions are transitory. The accepted meaning of the word "book" today may change into something entirely unrecognizable to today's readers. The same may hold true for any of the definitions we've just discussed. Technology, particularly technology involving computers and the Internet, is a moving target, and the target is moving fast.

But some things won't change, although the names for them might. Your writing, for instance, whether you call it *content, digital files* or *e-books,* will remain what it has always been: the concrete creation based on the thoughts you, and only you, have dreamed up.

And the way that writing reaches your readers, whether we call them *print books,* or *print-on-demand books,* or *e-books,* will still be nothing more than the thing that is read (well, unless somebody is doing something with telepathy we aren't aware of).

You still have to write. Readers still have to read. New ways for that to happen may be dreamed up on a moment's notice, but the essential transaction will remain the same, no matter how many new and strange methods of accomplishing it come to pass or how many new and strange words we conjure up to describe them.

When blind Homer rose beside a campfire and began to sing his tales of mighty heroes and mightier gods, no doubt he would have been completely unable to imagine his words, translated by the Gutenberg Project, rushing around the globe at the speed of light.

But it doesn't matter whether he could or not. The truth he knew—and that you know, deep in your writer's bones as well—is this: The song must be sung. Ears must hear it.

The digital revolution will spawn its own Homers, and their songs will be heard around a campfire that is global in scope.

And who knows? Maybe you'll be one of them.

CHAPTER EIGHTEEN

FINDING A FORMAT TO REACH THE MOST READERS

A writer dies and St. Peter asks, "Would you rather go to heaven or to hell?"

Thinking this may be a trick question, the writer says, "Let me do a little research first."

In the fiery pits, she finds row upon row of writers chained to their desks and immersed up to their waist in steaming lava. As they pound away at ancient manual Remingtons with sticky keys, they're whipped with thorny lashes.

"Tell you what," says the writer. "Let's have a looksee at heaven."

Just off the boulevards paved with gold, she finds row upon row of writers chained to their desks and immersed up to their waist in steaming lava. As they pound away at ancient manual Remingtons with sticky keys, they're whipped with thorny lashes.

"What the hey!" says the writer. "This is as bad as hell."

The clouds part, and a blazing beam of light lances down and pins the writer in its blinding glare.

"Hardly," booms a majestic voice. "Here, you get published."

James Stevens-Arce, author of the prize-winning *Soulsaver*, www. stevens-arce.com, took this anonymous joke from the Internet and cleaned it up a bit. The point is simple: Heaven is on the World Wide Web because *you get published*!

You don't need an agent. You don't have to submit to even one publisher, let alone dozens. You won't be getting any rejection letters. None of the well-known barriers to getting published in the traditional manner will stand in your way—which makes it all the more important that you take care, as discussed in chapters thirteen and fourteen, to present your work as well as you possibly can, since nobody else will be making sure you do so. But once you've decided your work is ready and you've decided to publish it yourself on your own Web page, what's next?

The technical issues involved in creating Web pages in the first place are lengthy, and we will discuss them in depth in section three. For now, we'll just take a quick look at the many formats you can use to publish on the Web—and elsewhere—and the advantages and disadvantages of each.

WWW FILE PRESENTATION FORMATS

- **TXT:** Plain ASCII text files.
- **RTF:** Rich text format.
- **DOC** (and others): Various word processor files.
- **HTML:** Hypertext markup language: the "language of the Web."

Text—The Most Basic Format

You've probably heard something to the effect that in order to publish on the World Wide Web, you need to know about a mysterious computer language called HTML, which stands for hypertext markup language. Sounds complicated, right? Well, if the mere thought of dealing with something that geeky makes you want to run screaming for the nearest old-fashioned typewriter, you do have an option that bypasses anything remotely technical. You can format your work as *plain text.* The technical term for this format is "ASCII text," which stands for American Standard Code for Information Interchange. What it boils down to is you can create your work on the most basic of computer text editors, then transfer it to your Web site, and other people can read it directly using any Web browser. You can spot a text file by the ".txt" at the end of the file name, as in: "somefile.txt."

A couple of caveats: Plain text is somewhat limited in how you can format your presentation. Basically, what you see in your text editor is what you will get: no page numbers, double spaces will have to be entered by hand (by using the "enter" key to move down two lines, instead of one), paragraph indentations are inserted by pressing the space bar and so on. However, plain text is a perfectly intelligible format, and one that can be read by the greatest number of methods. You can read it directly from a Web page, or you can download a text file from a Web site and read it with a basic computer text editor, a full-featured word processor or anything in between.

Project Gutenberg, which is to date the largest publisher of electronic texts in the history of the world, presents all of its offerings in text format, since the goal of the project is to make its works available and accessible to the largest number of readers possible.

It's a bit more work to properly format your work as plain text—and you won't be able to do any fancy presentation this way—but if the widest possible readership is your goal, you may want to consider this most basic of formats.

Make My Text Rich, Please

Let's say you want to stay reasonably basic, but you'd like a bit more control over how your work appears. Much of what we noted about plain text format also applies to what is called *rich text format,* more commonly known by its acronym, RTF. RTF was created by the Microsoft Corporation in an effort to provide a "platform independent" text standard (that means you can read it whether you're using Windows or MacOS, and whether you're using a Mac, a Sun computer, an Intel machine, a Palm Handheld and many others).

RTF can be read by most (though not all) text editors and word processors. It does, however, preserve much more of the layout you create for your work. Page numbers, automatic paragraph indentations, line spacing and so on will all appear as you created them originally using a word processor. Otherwise, you have most of the portability and accessibility of plain text. Think of RTF as a more sophisticated and flexible version of plain text. Files in this format (characterized by the filename type "somefile.rtf") can be read directly from a Web site by most major browsers, with no need for any knowledge or use of HTML coding. However, you should keep in mind that while Microsoft's Internet Explorer will read RTF files directly, older versions of Netscape require a free "plug-in" (software that gives Netscape additional capabilities) to do likewise. You can obtain this plug-in from the Netscape site, www.net scape.com. The latest versions of Netscape do read RTF files directly, with no additions necessary.

Document Files

Microsoft Word, in its various releases, is currently the most popular full-featured word processor in the world. Its standard format for document names is: "somefile.doc." An MS Word document file may be formatted and presented in an almost unlimited number of ways, giving the author an enormous amount of control over precisely how the finished product appears. And yes, you can put a Word DOC file on a Web page without bothering with HTML.

However, you should keep in mind that this is a *proprietary* format, owned and created by Microsoft for use with Microsoft products.

Microsoft's Web browser, Internet Explorer, will read these files seamlessly. Netscape has to call another program, usually Microsoft Word, in order to read them. Other browsers may take different approaches or simply be unable to read Word DOC files at all.

A further twist is that the .doc file extension is not proprietary. Both Corel WordPerfect and WordStar also use the same extension, and without attempting to open a "somefile.doc" there is no way to know in advance what you're dealing with. This can result in a fair amount of confusion and frustration on the part of the would-be reader. To be frank, confusion and frustration are not usually the state of mind authors wish their readers to be in when they first approach their work.

This is not to say that you should automatically avoid proprietary word processor formats, especially since they do give the author such great control over presentation. You should keep in mind, though, that such formats are by their nature less than a mass-market approach to presenting your work.

HTML Made Easy

If you intend to publish your own work using the World Wide Web, ask yourself what is the most widely used format for presentation *on* the Web? The answer? HTML *is* the standard for presenting content on the Web.

We touched on the history of the Web earlier, but to recap (from his home page at www.w3.org/People/Berners-Lee/Overview .html): "In 1989, while working at CERN, the European Particle Physics Laboratory, Tim Berners-Lee invented the World Wide Web, an Internet-based hypermedia initiative for global information sharing. He wrote the first Web client (browser-editor) and server in 1990."

This Web browser was designed to read text files modified with HTML, which he invented at the same time. All in all, quite a prodigious performance for one man. If you're thrilled, as a writer, that you are now able to publish your work with minimal effort in such a way that people all over the globe can read it cheaply and easily, you might want to send a thank-you note to Mr. Berners-Lee.

OK, so what *is* an HTML file? Nothing more, really, than a text file with "instruction tags" (also in text) placed here and there to tell a browser how to display the file in certain ways.

Here's a sample.

<p> in 1989 he invented the <a href=".../../TheProject.htm l"> World Wide Web</a>, an internet-based hypermedia initiative for global information sharing. while working at <a href="http://www.cern.ch/"> CERN</a>, the European Particle Physics Laboratory. He wrote the <a href="World-WideWeb.html"> first Web client (browser-editor)</a> and server in 1990.</p>

This is the actual HTML source code from the statement on Berners-Lee's Web page, summarized on page 87. See all those strange bits of text inside the angle brackets, like <this>? Those are called HTML *tags*. They are text instructions that tell any Web browser to do something with the text they modify. For instance, the tag <p> indicates that a new paragraph begins at that point. When a Web browser opens an HTML file and finds a <p>, it knows to format the following text with a double blank line to separate it from the preceding text.

HTML coding can get considerably more complicated than this, depending on how much control you want to exert over presentation of your text, but the basic principle remains: HTML is plain text modified with tags that tell a browser how to present that text.

As a plain text file, an HTML file has all the basic advantages we mentioned previously that apply to text: It is highly portable. Any text editor can "read" it—although you'll see all those pesky tags along with everything else. It is only when you read an HTML file with a Web browser that the tags become invisible. However, *any* Web browser can read *any* properly created HTML file. Once again, this format is "platform independent," just like plain text. If your computer setup, no matter what it is, can run a Web browser program, it can read an HTML file.

Because of the ubiquity of HTML on the World Wide Web and because of this platform-independent advantage, we strongly recommend that if you intend to e-publish on your own Web page, you do so in the HTML format. In the next chapter, we'll discuss the various possibilities for your work that can be accomplished by using HTML.

CHAPTER NINETEEN

AMAZING THINGS YOU CAN DO WITH HTML FORMATS

If you think of an HTML text file as a kind of pudding or cake, you can imagine that it might be possible to add some chunks of fruit or nuts to the batter, right? Well, you can. These nontext items are called "embedded objects." They can be something as simple as picture files or, slightly more complicated, sound files.

What this means is that you can design your HTML files to display pictures along with the text that appears in a Web browser. Or you could add (embed) a file that causes the browser to play a sound when it opens an HTML page that has a sound file embedded in the text. This is the capability that lets you design Web pages that look very much like magazine pages, complete with full-color illustrations. It also lets you add a "cover" to your book, if you so desire. And while most people don't usually think of a book as needing a sound track like a movie, if *you* think that's what your book needs, you can do it.

Hypertext

Leaving aside the reams of technical jargon about the World Wide Web, you only need to understand one thing about its structure:

The Web is a network capable of linking anything or everything to everything else on the network.

This is done by means of *hypertext links*. The links consist of the computer addresses of the material you want to link to. When you click on a link, your Web browser opens up the material residing at that address, wherever it may be.

You can link to a different part of your own book. Or you can link to some other text, picture, audio or video material on a computer thousands of miles away. Right away you can see some startling advantages to being able to do this. For instance, you might have a table of contents for your work, with each entry in the table hyperlinked to the beginning of the section listed. Click on the link in the table of contents, and go directly to the proper page. You could do the same thing with footnotes and indexes. If you write fiction, you might have created a large glossary of special words or a detailed section of history or character information. With hypertext, you can link character names (as they appear in the book) to individual sections about those characters.

And, of course, you might create links in one book to other books you've written, including links to where the interested reader can download and/or buy those books. That's a pretty cool notion, don't you think?

Hypertext is only one more tool made possible by the digital revolution, but it is a very powerful tool. For now, just keep it in mind as one more amazing option for you, the e-writer and e-publisher.

CHAPTER TWENTY

FORMATTING FOR HANDHELD E-BOOK READERS

We've covered a lot of information on formats in the past few chapters, but deciding what to format your e-book in is important so you meet the needs of your potential readers and make it as easy as possible for them to read your work. This means trying to anticipate any problems they may have in doing so. And remember, the more formats you make your work available in, the better for all your readers.

Certainly, if you want your book available on the Web, you should have a version of your book in HTML format, if only because the large majority of users will most likely prefer to read your work in their browser. However, for those who prefer to download your writing to their own computer and then "massage" it (which means to reformat it into something they prefer), you would want a plain text version available.

Some readers have become accustomed to using one of the "reader software" applications, such as Microsoft Reader or Adobe eBook Reader, which use, respectively, the .lit and .pdf formats. The popularity of these two formats will continue to grow, if only because the huge companies supporting them will market them vigorously in the future. So you should definitely consider using them. Let's discuss your options regarding these two formats.

Microsoft Reader Format

Microsoft Reader uses the LIT format. Sounds mysterious, right? Well, it isn't really. It's just another format, like TXT (for text) or DOC (for several word processors, primarily MS Word and Corel WordPerfect) that we talked about in chapter eighteen. A text editor can make a TXT file. MS Word can create a DOC file. So what makes a LIT file?

You might suspect that Microsoft Reader could convert a file to LIT automatically, but, unfortunately, it doesn't work that way. MS Reader only *reads* LIT files. It doesn't *write* (create) them. However, Microsoft anticipated the problem and provided a free "plug-in" (a computer program that adds capabilities to another program) for Microsoft Word. This plug-in allows you to work in Word's DOC format but convert the result to a LIT file. You can also use this feature as a converter for work you've already written, even if the writing was done in a non-MS Word format, as long as Word can open your original file. For instance, Word opens Corel WordPerfect files. Once such a file is opened, it can be saved as a Word DOC file, and that DOC file can then be reopened and converted to a LIT file, which can be read by Microsoft Reader.

Your intrepid authors took this MS Word plug-in for a test drive around the computer block. We downloaded it from Microsoft and installed it. The installation was simply a matter of clicking a few times on the proper buttons in the installation program. The plug-in installed without a hitch and added a new button to the bar at the top of Microsoft Word. We then opened a book we'd previously formatted as a Word document but laid out for printing in the normal quality paperback design. Once this document was open, we clicked on the Reader conversion button. The program went to work, asked us to enter a title for the book and then did the conversion and created a new LIT file.

Formatting for Handheld E-Book Readers

We then opened this LIT file with the Microsoft Reader program itself, and we have to say, we were surprised. The result kept all of the fonts and formatting that were in the original document but presented the LIT version in a format more or less indistinguishable from that of a printed page.

In other words, we were impressed both at the ease of use of the converter and at the results when using Microsoft Reader. Unfortunately, it is our approval that makes our regrets about Microsoft's Reader conversion utility more poignant: It isn't for everybody.

In order for the conversion to work, you must have the following system requirements met. These requirements are from the Microsoft download site for the Read-in Microsoft Reader add-in (www.microsoft.com/ebooks/tools/make_authors.asp):

- Microsoft Word 2000
- Pentium 75 or higher microprocessor
- Microsoft Windows® 98 Second Edition, Microsoft Windows NT® 4, Microsoft Windows 2000 Professional, Microsoft Windows 2000 Server and Windows ME operating systems
- 16 MB RAM
- Approximately 1 MB free hard disk space
- Microsoft Internet Explorer 4.01 with Service Pack 1 or later
- VGA or higher resolution monitor and video card capable of displaying more than 256 colors
- Microsoft mouse or compatible pointing device

The biggest concern about these requirements is the necessity of having a computer that uses the Windows 2000 operating system. What if you don't have a new machine? Well, unless and until Microsoft chooses to release a version of this conversion utility that works with other operating systems, you really don't have much of a choice. You will have to decide whether you want to spend the time, money and effort to install Windows 2000 on your computer, or, if not, you'll have to forego using the conversion program.

Are you doomed? Do you have to invest in Microsoft's latest and greatest operating system in order to publish your book in Microsoft Reader format?

Not at all! In fact, you don't even need to own a computer running any sort of Microsoft software. All you need is some sort of machine capable of running a Web browser—whether Windows, Mac, Unix, Linux, it doesn't matter, as long as you can access eBookExpress at www.ebookexpress.com.

This is one of the niftier Web gadgets we've ever seen. On this Web site, you'll find a page that allows you to turn almost any file format into a LIT file for Microsoft Reader. Best of all, it is entirely free!

Follow the simple directions you'll find there: Type in the name of the book, the name of the author and click on the "browse" button to locate the file you want to convert on your own computer. Then click on the button named "Click to Publish." That's all there is to it.

Be warned, however: If you have a standard 56k modem, the process could take a long time. This is because the Web site copies the file you want to convert from your computer to its server site—which means the larger the file and the slower the connection, the longer the wait.

Once the Web site has copied your file, it then performs the conversion to LIT format and notifies you when it is done. You then click another button on the site to transfer the new LIT file back to your own computer—and once again, if you are running a slow connection, this will take a while.

However, in the end, you'll have your book in LIT format, ready to view in Microsoft Reader and at no cost to you except for the time you spend waiting for converted files to go back and forth.

We highly recommend using this Web site to convert your files into an e-book format.

Adobe eBook Reader Format

The Adobe Corporation has created a new reader, which it calls
Adobe eBook Reader, specifically designed for electronic publishing, and, just as Adobe did with its Acrobat Reader (its basic .pdf
file reader), it is giving eBook Reader away.

There are millions of machines that already have some version of
the Acrobat Reader installed. If history is any indication, there will
shortly be a large number of machines with Adobe eBook Reader
installed as well. Most of the major publishing houses are already
supporting both Adobe eBook Reader and Microsoft Reader. This will
only serve to increase the popularity of these two e-book platforms, so
you will probably want to make sure you e-publish your book in PDF
format as well as Microsoft's LIT format.

The easiest and most straightforward way to go about this is to
purchase Adobe Acrobat, the program Adobe created to make and
convert PDF files. This is the gold standard of PDF software and
is priced accordingly. Adobe's list price for this software is around
$250. You can buy it online from Adobe at www.adobe.com/produ
cts/acrobat.main.html.

Adobe makes a host of other products that can create PDF files.
If you are interested in laying out your e-book with the same tool
used by thousands of professional and technical writers (all those
documents that came with your computer and software that you
don't read were probably made with this program), you should
look into Adobe FrameMaker. You can use this software package
to create beautifully finished literary creations, control every aspect
of your presentation, include all manner of illustrations and generally create a book as perfect as anything you will find in print. And
you can save your finished creations as PDF files, if you wish. Of
course, it will cost you. Adobe FrameMaker 6.0, the current release,
lists on the Adobe site at $799. Still, for those of you who enjoy
getting as deeply involved with how your book looks as you do in

writing the book itself, this may be just the thing. You can find out more about FrameMaker at www.adobe.com/products/framemaker/main.html.

Adobe offers several different publishing and presentation solutions. Adobe PageMaker, for instance, offers almost as many options as FrameMaker (including the ability to save in PDF) and, at $499, it costs substantially less. See it at www.adobe.com/products/pagemaker/main.html.

All of the Adobe programs we mention here are available for both Windows and the Mac.

OK. We can hear you patting your wallet and moaning softly. Isn't there any cheaper way to make PDF files? Maybe even something free?

Not exactly. But close.

The good folks at Dane Prairie Systems, LLC (www.daneprairie.com) have created a nifty little conversion utility called Win2PDF. Once installed on your computer, it acts like a printer. Any document you open can be "printed" to this utility, which will then convert the result into a PDF file. This is a very basic conversion and doesn't let you do anything fancy like adding security permissions (we'll discuss those in a later chapter), but it will get your book into the PDF format, which is readable in both Acrobat Reader and Adobe eBook Reader.

A couple of drawbacks: This program only works under Windows, not Mac, and it demands either Windows NT or Windows 2000. The authors state on their Web site that they will be supporting Microsoft's next operating system, which will replace Windows ME, called Windows XP. But you Windows 95, 98 and ME users will have to try something else. The program can be downloaded from the Web site we just mentioned. It costs $35, and for basic PDF conversion, we consider it well worth the price.

Now for you Mac people. At the Jim Walker's Software Source Web site (www.jwwalker.com) you can find a program called

PrintToPDF, which operates almost identically to the Win2PDF software and is compatible with MacOS7-9. This one costs $20, and we recommend it as well for simple PDF conversions.

Now, for those of you whose PDF conversion needs we haven't yet addressed, here's the solution that should work for just about everybody. Not surprisingly, it comes from Adobe.

Type into the address window in your Web browser the address: http://createpdf.adobe.com.

This will take you to a Web page on the Adobe site that allows you to upload files from your own computer to the Adobe site for conversion to PDF. It works in exactly the same way as eBook Express's converter page for Microsoft Reader LIT files: Just plug in the name of the file you want to convert, click the conversion button and wait. Remember, if you have a slow Internet connection, you may wait a long time.

A few caveats: Unlike the eBook Express site, this one isn't free. You must register first in order to use it at all. Registration entitles you to convert three files free in order to test everything. However, to perform more than three conversions, you have to sign up for a subscription. You can pay by the month for $10, or by the year, which costs $100. Remember, you don't have to use the site to convert multiple copies of your book. A single copy will do. You can make as many copies of that file as you wish, once you've downloaded it back to your computer.

This site is no substitute for Adobe's much more powerful stand-alone products like Acrobat or PageMaker. However, it will let you convert the following files to PDF:

- **Microsoft® Office:** Word (.doc), Publisher (.pub), PowerPoint (.ppt), Excel (.xls), Rich Text Format (.rtf), Text (.txt)
- **Adobe Formats:** Illustrator® (.ai), InDesign™ (.indd), Frame-Maker® (.fm), PageMaker® (.pm, .pm6, .p65), Photoshop® (.psd)
- **Corel WordPerfect Office Formats:** WordPerfect (.wpd)

- **Adobe PostScript® Formats:** PostScript (.ps, .prn), Encapsulated PostScript (.eps)
- **Image Formats:** Windows bitmap (.bmp), GIF (.gif), JPEG (.jpg), PCX (.pcx), PNG (.png), RLE (.rle), TIFF (.tif)

One benefit of using a PDF format is that you can add security features to your PDF files to prevent others from copying, changing or printing your work. For some authors, this could be quite important, as we explained more thoroughly in our discussion of digital rights management in chapter eleven.

Not free, but not bad, either. We recommend it.

CHAPTER TWENTY-ONE

ALTERNATE OPPORTUNITIES FOR E-PUBLISHING

No matter what sort of connection your readers have to the Internet—even high-speed cable or DSL (Digital Subscriber Line)—nothing is as fast as having your book on their own computers. Therefore, it's in your best interest to offer readers some way to get the book onto their computers once and have done with it.

One of the best ways to accomplish this task is by using an old method that is an integral part of the original Internet called "file transfer protocol" (FTP). FTP allows you to download files from any location directly to your own machine. Already, many e-publishers, rather than forcing would-be readers to struggle with slow connections each time they wish to view an author's Web page, are using FTP to let the reader download the entire book file in one fell swoop, so it can be read anytime and at the full speed of the reader's own personal computer.

ZIP Disks

There are even ways to "compress" files to make them faster to download. The most popular way is the common "ZIP" file format. Popularized by such "file compression utilities" as WinZip (www

.winzip.com) and PKZip (www.pkware.com), ZIP format is an easy and efficient way to "package" your book so you can spare your readers the ordeal of endless, time-consuming downloads.

While ZIP format is very popular in the United States, the Internet is a global affair, and other places have developed different preferences. In Europe, the TAR and GZIP formats are popular. The Macintosh computer also uses a somewhat different format called HQX. For a good rundown of all the major compression formats, complete with links to in-depth discussions of each, check out The Diffuse Project's excellent Guide to Data Compression File Formats at www.diffuse.org/zip.html.

CD-ROMS

Remember what we're dealing with here: a *book* transformed into a *digital file*. Now, this file just happens to be ideally suited to shipping all over the world, via the Internet, at the speed of light. But as we've noted, your readers' computers could be pretty darned slow, especially if the doorway into their computers is through one of those painfully stodgy modems that make those weird squawking noises.

The people who make and sell software have been dealing with the problem of speed for quite some time now. Software has almost always consisted of fairly large files that took a long time to download, by whatever standard was considered speedy at any given period of computer and Internet development. The solution to the problem was straightforward: You didn't download software when you bought it. You went into a store and bought a disk with the software already on it, then took that home and installed from there.

With the advent of DSL and cable modems, which brought much faster download speeds to those lucky enough to be able to obtain and afford such things, a fair amount of software is now actually delivered over the Internet. But for the major programs like Office Suites, image programs and many others, even with a

DSL or cable connection, it still isn't really practical to download several hundred megabytes of files. So you use the Web to shop for goods, even to pay for them; but when push comes to shove, the seller still puts a disk of some sort into your hand and lets you take it from there.

Today, the most popular form these disks take is the CD-ROM, a shiny plastic disk about the size of a coffee cup saucer. Almost all personal computers sold today come with a CD-ROM drive included, and most software is sold in this format.

Now, even a four-hundred-page novel, in text format, won't make a file much larger than one megabyte. For someone with a DSL connection, it's a matter of only a few seconds to download something that size, and even with a standard modem, it can be done in a few minutes.

But what if you have your book in some format other than plain text? Or you've added pictures or even sound? If that's the case, it won't take much before you've got files too big to download quickly and easily.

And even if you have a nice, slim text file, there is something to be said for your reader being able to get the digital equivalent of a print book—that is, as a tangible item like a disk, the same way folks buy music compact discs.

A further advantage is the ability to put several books on a single CD-ROM—just in case one of your readers would like to own everything you've written.

Luckily for you, you can accommodate your fans. Transferring files to a CD-ROM—a process that used to take hundreds of thousands of dollars of equipment and specialized expertise—can now be done almost automatically with equipment you can add to your computer for less than two hundred dollars.

The process is called "burning" a CD. You can buy inexpensive units called "CD-RW" (Compact Disc Read Write) drives that allow you to both play back CDs as well as copy your own files onto blank disks. Special software is usually supplied with these CD-RW drives to let you easily make your own data CDs. There are several popular programs made for this purpose, including Adaptec Corporation's Easy CDWriter (for Windows-based computers) and Toast, a similar program made by the same company for the Mac. Check these programs out at www.adaptec.com. Hewlett-Packard makes both hardware CD-RW drives as well as software for them. See their latest products at www.hpcdwriter.com/products/internal_cdwriter.asp.

DVD—The Wave of the Future

DVD is an acronym for "Digital Versatile Disks." They are much like CDs, except they are smaller and can contain much more data.

At this point, the technology for making or "burning" DVDs on your home computer is expensive. These drives (called DVD-RAM drives) can cost upwards of a thousand dollars. Further, while almost every machine these days is equipped with a CD-ROM drive that can "read" CDs, DVD drives are rare in home computers (though rapidly becoming more common on new computers).

It is likely that eventually DVD technology will overtake and then replace CD systems. However, that time has not yet come. We would recommend that you wait for this DVD technology to mature a bit, come down in price and become more commonly used before considering using it as an e-publishing medium.

OH, Enough of This

Internet and World Wide Web. HTML, plain text, rich text, proprietary formats. CD-ROMs and DVD-RAMs. It's enough to make your head spin! What does all this geek talk have to do with writing, you might wonder?

Nothing, really. But it has everything to do with *publishing*, at least with e-publishing. We include it to give you, the writer who wants to become an e-publisher, some basic understanding of the issues involved in why, where and how you can present your work in the new digital world.

And if you find all of this a bit overwhelming, well, take heart. The same technology that sounds so complicated is already being used to make the stuff you actually want to do much simpler.

Remember the basic notion: E-books are books in digital format, and e-publishing is the method you choose to present those e-books to your potential readers.

So let's get down to specifics. You've got your magnum opus polished to perfection, and you're ready to show it—to e-publish it—to the world. So how do you do that?

To learn how, check out the next two sections, Self-Publishing on the Web and Working With Others to E-Publish Your E-Book.

PART THREE

Self-Publishing on the Web

CHAPTER TWENTY-TWO

GETTING ON THE INFORMATION SUPERHIGHWAY AND STAYING THERE

As we enter the twenty-first century, there are about 134 million Internet users in the United States and tens of millions more in the rest of the world. Odds are, you are one of them. But for those of you who aren't, let's take a quick look at the most basic of Internet issues: how to get connected to the Net and how to use that connection to enter the realm of the World Wide Web.

Modems

First, you need a modem to turn your telephone line into a line to the Internet. A basic telephone line connection will use an *analog* modem, either a card that inserts into your computer or a small box that sits outside your computer. Almost every computer sold in the past few years is equipped with an internal modem; but if your computer is older or for some reason isn't so equipped, then you'll have to buy a modem. Which to buy? The *external* modems, little boxes outside your computer, are easy to set up; however, they do cost a bit more. Expect to pay from thirty to a hundred dollars for an internal modem and twenty or thirty dollars more for the external variety. In either case, make sure you get a modem rated at 56k speed, which is the current standard.

Your Connection to the Internet

Once you have your modem set up and running, you'll need to arrange for your connection to the Internet. Though it would be nice, you can't simply plug your modem into a phone outlet and start surfing the Web. You'll need to open an account with an *ISP* (Internet Service Provider). The general way things work is that you connect your computer via its modem to a computer owned by the ISP, and the ISP connects to the Internet.

America Online, Inc. (AOL) is an ISP that currently connects more than twenty-five million people to the Internet. This huge company specializes in serving folks who know little or nothing about technical issues and who would like to keep it that way. Generally, if you have a computer with a working modem and a CD-ROM drive, all you need is a disk from AOL. Put the disk in your drive, follow the directions and you can be connected to the Internet in less than five minutes.

Another possibility is your local telephone company. Almost all phone companies offer Internet service. The same is true for all the nationwide long distance services. Just call up customer service and ask.

Finally, there are large independent ISPs, like Earthlink, Microsoft Network and CompuServe. You'll find them listed in your local telephone directory. If you are interested in a smaller provider, perhaps a regional or even a local operation, check out CNET's ISP Comparison Service at http://webisplist.internetlist.com.

Expect to pay about twenty dollars a month for unlimited (that means twenty-four hours a day, seven days a week) access. However, you might also want to look at the *free* service providers. These services don't charge you anything to get hooked up. Sound too good to be true? Well, it is, unless you love seeing a lot of advertising on your computer screen. So-called "free" ISPs pay their bills by plastering various sorts of ads on your computer. Further, we don't think they offer much in the way of service or dependability (several have recently gone out of business) and so, at this time, we don't recommend them.

Even if you don't plan to e-publish on the World Wide Web, you'll still want to take advantage of the Web for other purposes—a "home page" for yourself (you can post your author picture there) and/or Web pages where you can promote and market your e-book.

Web Space—The Home for Your Home Page

All major ISPs offer "Web space" to their clients, generally as part of the basic sign-up package. This Web space is nothing more than a certain amount of space on the hard drive of a computer owned by the ISP, called a "Web server." Anybody on the Internet can connect to this Web server and view Web pages that are stored there.

The amount of space you get can vary from ISP to ISP, but usually from two to thirty megabytes are included in the standard monthly fee. Depending on the length of your e-book as well as on the size of the other files you use to create your personal Web site, you may need to purchase more space, although generally you won't.

Know Your Download Costs

One other factor to keep in mind regarding your choice of ISP and Web space: What if your book turns out to be enormously popular? What if tens, even hundreds, of thousands of frenzied readers want to download the book from your site?

If this happens, you could be looking at some extra costs. Most service providers allow you a certain minimum amount of "traffic" on your Web site before charging you extra. The traffic is usually measured by the size of the total download from your site over a month. It works like this: Let's say your immensely popular e-book is a file that is one megabyte in size. Each time that book is downloaded, you use up one megabyte of your basic allowance. However, this isn't all there is to it. Your Web page itself is included. Let's say you have lots of pictures (your lovingly designed book cover, for instance), a background sound file that plays each time your Web page is accessed and whatever other files you've used to generally spiff things up. Each time a surfer "reads" your Web page, all of the files that make up that page are downloaded (copied) to that surfer's machine. If the total of the files used to create your Web page amounts to, say, three megabytes, that is how much is downloaded *each* time somebody looks at your page on their computer.

It can add up very quickly for a really popular site. One major ISP offers 5 *gigabytes* (1 gigabyte equals 1,000 megabytes) of downloads with their basic package and charges ten cents for each megabyte over that limit.

Sounds like a lot, doesn't it? But take a look at that 3 megabyte Web page you've designed. If you divide 5,000 megabytes (5 gigabytes) by 3 (the size of your Web page), you end up with 1,667. That means after 1,667 people merely *look* at your Web page, you will be over your limit. Each time somebody new looks at your page, you'll owe an additional thirty cents (ten cents per megabyte times three).

So what's a few dimes between friends, you ask? Well, at that rate for "extra" usage, each thousand viewers over your limit will cost you $333.00. Ten thousand viewers will add a nifty $3,333.00 to your bill. Ten thousand page views for a popular site is quite low. Major Web portals like Yahoo! receive hundreds of millions of page views every month.

Now, your site might not become so popular that you suddenly find yourself receiving huge monthly bills from your ISP. Nevertheless, if you are successful in employing the marketing tools we discuss later in this book, you may find yourself staring in disbelief at your monthly credit card bill. There are several ways to protect yourself against these kinds of nasty surprises. The most obvious ways are to avoid creating those bloated 3-megabyte Web pages and to shop around for the best deals you can find on download costs.

Be warned: Most ISPs don't make it easy to find out this information, so it's best to make sure you ask your customer service representative about download costs and limits *before* you sign up for service.

Learn a lesson from Stephen King. He posted a financial statement about his online serial novel *The Plant*. (Go take a look. It makes for interesting reading, www.stephenking.com/PlantNumbe rs_010101.html). One of the expense listings is for "Web hosting and maintenance." That's the part that covers what we've just discussed. The total is $102,849.59. Stephen King can afford that kind of cost, but can you?

Well, if you are lucky enough to sell as many e-books as King does, yes, you can. But these extravagant fees are still something to keep in mind. Expenses are an integral—and unavoidable—part of any business, including the business of e-publishing. Make sure you keep them as low as you possibly can.

CHAPTER TWENTY-THREE

SETTING UP YOUR DOMAIN NAME

What's in a name? Shakespeare had Juliet wonder to Romeo. Juliet went on to discuss roses, while we must turn to other fields—your name, for instance, and how it relates to something called a "domain name."

On the Web, everything has a name. This is how one computer is able to find any other computer. In fact, the address of any given Web page is called a "URL," which stands for "Universal Resource Locator." A URL is actually a combination of a name and an address.

What is your name worth to you? What does it mean to you? It identifies you, and it is a way for others to find you among the billions of other citizens of Planet Earth. Combine your name with your address, and the combination denotes you, and you alone. It's the same with names on the Web.

Leaving aside the technical details, there is one kind of name used on the Web that can—and should—be of great interest to you. It is called a domain name.

Let's look at one famous example: the domain name for the famous Web site known as "Yahoo!" The basic URL for Yahoo! is www.yahoo.com. Yahoo! (the Web site) uses, oddly enough, the domain name "yahoo" to identify itself to all other computers. Now, every Web page of the thousands of separate Web pages on the Yahoo! site has an individual address that is a subset of the yahoo domain name, as in: www.yahoo.com/setofpages/anotherset/oneparticularpage.html. But when computers go looking for that one page, *first* they look for the Yahoo domain.

Did you know that you can purchase your very own domain name and you can make it anything you want, as long as somebody else hasn't already purchased the name you want? Let's say that your name is Geraldine Author. You could buy a domain name called geraldineauthor.com. Your own name would become your unique address all over the world and the World Wide Web—almost as if you could live in a town in the nondigital world also called by your name. On the Web, your domain is your home town, your address, your castle.

POSSIBLE DOMAIN SUFFIXES

There were originally six different types of "top level" domain names. Each one is designated by a three letter suffix that follows the domain name itself. The six are listed here. What's the difference? Each type denotes a specific sort of site.

- **Net:** Used for network sites like Internet Service Providers.
- **Org:** Used for nonprofit sites like foundations.
- **Edu:** Educational sites; colleges, universities.
- **Mil:** Military sites; e.g., the U.S. Army.
- **Gov:** Government sites; the White House, for instance.
- **Com:** Commercial sites. This is the one you want.

Here's how you go about buying some Web acreage named after yourself.

Domain names are administered by a worldwide organization called the Internet Corporation for Assigned Names and Numbers, more commonly known by the acronym ICANN. ICANN allows certain other entities to actually issue domain names on their behalf. The oldest, biggest and most popular of these entities is called the

Network Solutions Company, a subsidiary of the VeriSign Corporation.

Go to Network Solutions's home page at www.networksolutions .com. You will be presented with a search engine into which you type the domain name you are interested in registering. In your case, perhaps something like yourname.com. The engine will then search through all registered domain names to see if the one you want has already been registered. If it hasn't, you will be transferred immediately to a new page that will let you immediately register and pay for your domain name. You can't really buy these names outright. What you do is "rent" them for a specific period of time. One year is minimum. At Network Solutions, you can pay in advance for up to ten years, however, if you don't want to have to renew your lease each year.

It doesn't cost much, either. You can get a basic package for a year for about thirty-five dollars. Just follow the directions, use your credit card and you should be set up with your own domain name in just a few minutes.

One last consideration: What if you plug your name into the search engine and find that someone else has already registered it? If your name is John Doe, that will likely be the case; and if someone else named John Doe has registered JohnDoe.com, there really isn't much you can do except contact Mr. Doe directly to see if he'd be willing to give up his domain and let you use it. However, you may find that your name has been registered by what are called "squatters." Squatters are people—or companies—who register names they believe might have potential value at some later date but don't intend to actually use those names. They intend to sell them, and they regard them as a form of investment. If you are unlucky enough to find that your own name has been registered by a squatter, probably the simplest solution is to see if a different form of your name might be available. For instance, if your name is Jane Aloysus Doe, and you wanted to register janedoe.com but found it already taken, check out janeadoe, or jadoe, or janealo, or even janealoysusdoe.

In reality, squatters register names they think somebody will want to pay for, and generally the names of "regular people" won't be seen as good investments—unless you are a regular person who just happens to be named Stephen King.

The Authors Guild recently took the issue to ICANN and won a ruling from that governing body to the effect that an author has a direct interest in her own name and stated that squatters who have no interest of their own must return such registrations to the author if so requested.

This probably won't affect you for a couple of reasons: First, as mentioned previously, unless you are reasonably well known, squatters probably won't be interested in your name. Second, this doesn't give even well-known authors blanket use of their names. If someone named Stephen King, who didn't happen to be the author, had registered that domain name for his own use and then used it, the horror writer would have no case. Domain names are distributed on a first-come, first-served basis. Still, it is nice to know that if you happen to fall into the category affected by the ICANN decision, you do have some recourse.

Domain Name Games

Congratulations! You've registered your name as your own domain on the World Wide Web. But though you've completed this important first step, that's not the end of it. At this point, all you have is a domain name. You still have to find some particular computer that will identify itself with your domain name so other computers can find your domain on the Web. This is called "domain hosting." You need somebody to host your own domain, because unless somebody does, you can't be a host yourself and invite others to

SOMETHING TO WATCH OUT FOR

In a perfect world, everybody would be honest, and nobody would try to take advantage of others. However, we don't live in such a world and, as has often been said, the Internet is a wild and wooly place, something like the old American West before the sheriff came to town. The Federal Trade Commission has issued a warning about fraud in the domain name game. We reproduce the article (found at www.ftc.gov/bcp/conline/pubs/alerts/domainalrt.htm) in full:

What's Dot and What's Not:
Domain Name Registration Scams

What's in a name? Plenty, if you want to register a Web site. A new scam is targeting would-be Web site owners by offering the opportunity to preregister new top-level domain names. Domain names, such as "ftc.gov," are the unique terms that enable Internet users to locate a specific Web site. The top-level domain is the final extension, such as ".com" or ".org."

According to the Federal Trade Commission (FTC), the nation's consumer protection agency, scam artists are taking advantage of the news that the Internet Corporation for Assigned Names and Numbers (ICANN) has made new top-level domains available to the public. These new domains are .aero, .biz, .coop, .info, .museum, .name, and .pro.

The FTC says consumers are getting fax and e-mail solicitations that offer a chance at a new top level domain name, for a fee, as soon as it becomes available. Some registration services are guaranteeing new top level domain names or promising preferential treatment in the registration process. But, the agency cautions, these offers may be misleading.

The FTC advises consumers to protect themselves by:

1. Avoiding any domain name pre-registration service that guarantees particular top-level domain names or preferential treatment in the assignment of new top-level domain names.

> 2. Avoiding doing business with people who send unsolicited faxes—
> regardless of the offer. Unsolicited faxes are illegal.
>
> 3. Staying on top of the news about top-level domain names at the
> ICANN Web site, www.icann.org.
>
> So, a word to the wise: Use the same care in registering a domain
> that you would in any other important business transaction.

your Web page for a nice cup of virtual tea and a quick read through your latest opus.

Who will host your virtual home?

Most likely, your ISP will be more than happy to do so. They'll even set up the technical information so other computers can find you. Of course, they will charge you for this—and prices can, and do, vary. Currently, you shouldn't have to pay more than a hundred dollars or so for this, depending on the bells and whistles you want them to add—like different e-mail boxes or larger Web space on their hard drives. If the tariff is much higher than this, refuse. It isn't necessary that your ISP host your domain. There are other companies that will be happy to do so, including Network Solutions, where you registered your name in the first place.

There are several sites that try to provide links to and information about hundreds of different hosting sites.

- Web Host Directory is one. See them at www.webhostdir.com. They offer an excellent search engine that allows you to look for sites within a certain price range or by the features offered.
- Host Search, at www.hostsearch.com offers a similar service.
- WebHosters.com, at www.webhosters.com (Isn't this domain name stuff fascinating?), offers a handy list of the largest, most popular hosting sites. Take a look at www.webhosters.com/top_hosts/host_spotlights/index.html for the index of these sites.

Keep in mind that what we have just discussed only touches the surface of the issues. One of the characteristics of the Web and the Internet is the overwhelming number of choices and solutions you can find on almost every technical or computer decision. We can't pretend to give you an in-depth discussion here, but what we have told you will at least get you started.

CHAPTER TWENTY-FOUR

RESOURCES FOR LEARNING HTML

O K, so now you've done your research and picked the best ISP for your needs. And you've set up your cozy domain in the wilds of the World Wide Web. Now it's time to create your very own Web page. And that means it's time to renew your recent acquaintance with that mysterious computer code: HTML.

The first question you might have is, "Can I do this weird stuff by myself, or do I need an army of experts or hundreds of dollars of software to do it for me?"

The short answer is yes, you can do it for yourself, with a bit of study and nothing more than the text editor included with your computer operating system. Remember that sample of HTML we showed you in chapter eighteen? Nothing more than text with a few "tags"—also in text, written inside a set of angle brackets, <like so>.

It's beyond the scope of this book to teach you HTML. However, we can point you to some places where you can go to learn it yourself.

As we've noted, the World Wide Web was invented by Tim Berners-Lee, and so was HTML, so where better might one go to learn about HTML than from the horse's mouth? We're talking about W3C, which is an acronym for the World Wide Web Consortium, which was also founded by Mr. Berners-Lee.

• W3C's Web site offers you up-to-date information about all things HTML, including tutorials on how to create the most basic Web pages with nothing but a simple text editor. There are also tutorials at the site for those who want to learn advanced techniques. To start, go to the following site: www.w3.org/MarkUp/Guide/

- The National Center for Supercomputing Applications (NCSA) at the University of Illinois at Urbana/Champaign also offers a complete (and free) primer on HTML, along with a wide selection of links to other HTML information. You can find their primer at http://archive.ncsa.uiuc.edu/General/Internet/WWW/HTMLPrimer.html.

- A third excellent source on the World Wide Web for information about HTML is Hotwired/Lycos's Webmonkey, which offers information and instruction for everybody from the basic amateur to the experienced pro. Visit Webmonkey at http://hotwired.lycos.com/webmonkey/authoring/html_basics/.

If you prefer to take your studies lying down, preferably curled up with a hot cappuccino and a print-on-paper book, you're in luck. Since the advent of the Web, authors have written hundreds of books explicating the mysteries of HTML. Here are several books we found to be useful in helping you learn how to design and build your own Web site using HTML, no matter what your level of knowledge of the subject might be. The Dummies and Idiots books take a more basic, step-by-step approach suitable for beginners; the remaining books, while still excellent for those just starting out, may be of even greater value to those who already have a bit of experience with HTML.

Many of these books are available at your local bookshop. All are currently available online from Amazon.com at www.amazon.com, and many will be on the shelves of your local library or can be obtained by your friendly librarian.

Learning Web Design: A Beginner's Guide to HTML, Graphics, and Beyond, by Jennifer Niederst and Richard Koman, published by O'Reilly & Associates, March 2001. Amazon.com's editorial review of this book says:

> In *Learning Web Design: A Beginner's Guide to HTML, Graphics, and Beyond,* author Jennifer Niederst shares the knowledge she's gained from years of Web design experience, both as a designer and as a teacher. This book starts from the very beginning—defining the Internet, the Web, browsers, and URLs—so you don't have to have any previous knowledge about how the Web works. Jennifer helps you build the solid foundation in HTML, graphics, and design principles that you need for crafting effective Web pages. She also explains the nature of the medium and unpacks the Web design process from conceptualization to the final result.

HTML Pocket Reference (Nutshell Handbook), by Jennifer Niederst, published by O'Reilly & Associates in 1999. This book, also by Ms. Niederst, provides the reader with a handy HTML "dictionary" of HTML tags. Amazon.com's review notes:

> The author of the best-selling *Web Design in a Nutshell,* Jennifer Niederst, delivers a concise guide to every HTML tag in this pocket reference. Each tag entry includes:—Detailed information on the tag's attributes—Browser support information, including Netscape Navigator, Microsoft Internet Explorer, Opera, and WebTV HTML 4.0 support information. . . . This pocket reference is targeted at Web designers and Web authors and is likely to be the most dog-eared book on every Web professional's desk.

Complete Idiot's Guide to Creating a Web Page, Fourth Edition, by Paul McFedries, published by Complete Idiot's Guide, 1999. A review from *Book News* said:

> A book/CD-ROM guide to creating a Web page, using a simple, lighthearted approach and step-by-step instructions. Chapters are in sections on creating a page, adding images and other details, working with style sheets, JavaScripts and Java Applets, page production, and Web page style. The CD-ROM contains HTML editors, graphics programs, graphics files, and sample Web pages.

HTML 4 for Dummies: Quick Reference (For Dummies), by Deborah S. Ray and Eric J. Ray, published by Hungry Minds, Inc., 2000. Amazon.com's editorial reviewers say:

> This guide is appropriate for those who just need to know enough HTML to get around or who want a convenient, quick reference for the little things they forgot. While far short of a complete course on HTML, this reference is much more than a mere cheat sheet. The signature lightheartedness of the For Dummies series can help make you comfortable if the giant HTML tomes are too daunting.

Just as your local university or community college offers courses in writing, they also very likely offer courses in HTML. Or there may be an adult learning center available that offers just what you need. Something to keep in mind: There are so many different ways to learn about HTML, and most of these can be learned for free or for the cost of a book or two, so don't get taken in by courses that cost hundreds, even thousands, of dollars. If you have to spend more than fifty dollars to learn HTML, you're paying too much. Don't do it.

Your Humble HTML Editor

OK, so you thought that learning HTML sounded like a good idea. But you looked at the online courses and peeked inside the books at your local bookstore, and you decided that even those deals supposedly for "dummies" or "idiots" look overwhelming. As far as you're concerned, the less you have to know about HTML, the better. Are you doomed to be locked out of the World Wide Web forever, your dreams of e-publishing on the Web dashed by a lack of geekitude?

Not at all. In fact, wouldn't it be nice to have a computer genius with you, showing you how to create your own Web page, doing all that incomprehensible HTML coding herself and otherwise holding your hand every step of the way?

Sure it would. And that text editor, or a reasonable facsimile, may be hiding in your computer right now. Do you have a version of Microsoft Word later than 1997, preferably Word 2000? How about Corel WordPerfect Office 2000 or the latest iteration of Sun's StarOffice Suite? If so, you're set. Just use one of these word processors/desktop publishers to lay out your Web page as if you were designing a magazine page, then save the result as an HTML file. That's it. Simple, easy and nearly instantaneous. We've mentioned these word processors previously, but in case you missed it, here is where to go for further information.

- **Microsoft Word 2000:** The Microsoft Corporation will be happy to tell you everything about the most popular word processor in the world, at www.microsoft.com/office/word/default.htm.
- **Corel WordPerfect Office 2000:** Once number one, now a major competitor, and costs a bit less, too. Go to www.corel.com.
- **StarOffice:** The new kid on the block from Sun Corporation, but just as powerful as the better-known flavors. StarOffice has one huge advantage over all the other big guys. It's free. Get yours at www.staroffice.com.

If you'd like to try something with a bit more firepower than a word processor, there are several *dedicated* HTML text editors. Dedicated means these software applications are designed specifically to create Web pages. They make creating even complicated Web sites a snap. If you can point-n-click and drag-n-drop, you can whip out a professional-looking Web page in less than an hour (maybe a lot less) with one of these programs. Two of the best known HTML text editors are Microsoft Front Page 2000 and Macromedia Dreamweaver 4.

Microsoft FrontPage 2000

This is the most popular HTML text editor out there. Some people seem to think it may be the best one, as well. In their *Computer Shopper* (www.zdnet.com/computershopper/) review of December 12, 2000, Dan Labriola and David English wrote: "Whether you want to create Dynamic HTML animations, integrate Microsoft Access databases into a Web page, or simply get a personal Web site up and running with a minimum of fuss, FrontPage supplies intuitive tools that make the job a cinch."

If you already use other Microsoft Office programs like Microsoft Word, an added advantage is the extensive integration between FrontPage 2000 and those applications. At around $135, the program isn't exactly cheap, but it isn't nearly as expensive as some of its competitors. Something else to keep in mind: FrontPage is not compatible with the Mac.

Macromedia Dreamweaver 4

Dreamweaver has been a major player in the Web authoring field for quite some time. This program offers advanced HTML text editing capabilities but is still fully capable of building a simple Web site without a lot of technical knowledge being necessary on the part of the user.

In *ZDNet Review* (www.zdnet.com), Jay Munro said, "While Dreamweaver isn't the perfect development environment . . . we still think it is the tool of choice for building clean, compatible Web sites. We like the overall ease of use and the new features like the JavaScript debugger, team support and layout mode. These features make it even more compelling if you are designing pages for a living, or just maintaining a site as the designated web master in your office."

Dreamweaver 4 is a bit more expensive than Microsoft's Front-Page. When we checked, we found prices in a range from $250 to $300. However, Dreamweaver is compatible with the Mac, and if you are a bit more technically inclined than the average user, you can take advantage of Dreamweaver's large number of advanced tools and capabilities.

There are dozens of other Web authoring, design and site-building packages out there. The field changes too rapidly for us to try to give you a complete survey. However, for the latest information, you can visit any Web site that offers software reviews. We recommend:

ZDNet Review's: www.zdnet.com/reviews/

CNET Editor's Choice: http://cnet.com/editorschoice/0-15505 83.html?tag=st.sw.8888.smpl.1550583.

Yahoo has links to an enormous number of reviews at http://dir.yahoo.com/Computers_and_Internet/Software/Reviews/.

Once you've decided what sort of software and methods you plan to use to create your Web page—rather like a carpenter deciding which tool to use to build a house—the next step is learning how to make your Web page look good. We'll show you the best resources for Web design in the next chapter.

CHAPTER TWENTY-FIVE

HOW YOU CAN BUILD A GREAT E-PUBLISHING WEB SITE

In a digital medium like the Web, you can present yourself almost any way you'd like to. Even if your personal "publishing house" in the real world consists of a table in your laundry room, that's not what the world will see on your Web page.

You can make your Web page as simple as a nearly blank piece of paper or as complicated and impressive as the General Motors site. It's up to you. But before you rush out to commission background music for your pages or have a friend shoot a half-hour video tour of the laundry room where you wrote your book, there are a few things you should keep in mind.

The most important is this: Your Web page is the first thing about you that the rest of the world sees. Make sure that what your visitors encounter is the best you can possibly offer. Just as your writing will compete with everything from Danielle Steele to the junior high kid down the block, your Web site, in a sense, is competing with every other site on the Internet. And remember: *You never get a second chance to make a first impression.*

Keep Your Download Times Lean and Mean

As we discussed, the speed at which somebody "surfs" the Internet is determined by their modem. Another term for this sort of speed is "bandwidth."

A WEB SITE SUCCESS STORY

When John Blumenthal's agent sent out the author's manuscript of *What's the Matter With Dorfman?* to major print publishers, the responses that came back were the kind that are familiar to all too many writers. Everybody loved the book. Nobody wanted to publish it.

Even more depressing was that Blumenthal, as author of four previously published humorous novels and Hollywood screenwriter of the hit comedy-thriller *Blue Streak*, had all the advantages most beginning writers assume means instant print publication: He was an established author with a good track record, a good agent and a book he knew from his own experience was certainly of publishable quality. Even his rejections confirmed that everybody liked the book. They just couldn't figure out how to sell it. Blumenthal decided to self-publish the novel and do the selling himself.

At this point, Blumenthal's experience with technical matters and the Web were minimal. He had no Web page at all and no idea how to go about getting one. But after reading some articles by e-publishing whiz M.J. Rose in *Wired Magazine*, he decided to self-publish *Dorfman* and realized that he would need some sort of presence on the Web in order to market the book. (You can see his page at www.whatswrongwithdorfman .com/index.html.)

With some excellent help and advice, Blumenthal created a Web site that follows all the basic principles of good Web design. It loads quickly, is easy to navigate, makes it very simple to buy the book and even has the added advantage of a domain name that leads search engines directly to the page. If you plug just the word "dorfman" into the Google.com search engine, Blumenthal's Web page is the third item that pops up.

So how did it turn out? *January Magazine* named *What's the Matter With Dorfman?* as one of the top fifty books of 2000. The book is available through every major online bookstore and in many chain and independent "brick-and-mortar" bookstores. Blumenthal is now into a third printing of the book with more than five thousand copies sold (at $11.95) in less than a year.

This is a success story even by traditional print publishing standards, and Blumenthal credits the Web site he created for *Dorfman* as being a large part of that success.

Think of bandwidth as a stream or brook. Call it a "datastream." The bigger the stream, the more water it can carry. The bigger the bandwidth, the more data it can carry. Really big streams are called "broadband" streams.

As we make the turn into the twenty-first century, nine out of ten connections to the Internet are made through sloooow 56k modems. Only one in ten lucky surfers is connected to the Net through broadband hookups, almost all either DSL or cable connections. And that means you want to design your site to be as fast to download as possible.

If a surfer tries to access your Web site and the little "wait" timer starts ticking . . . and ticking . . . and ticking, likely as not, your potential visitor will go looking for a Web site a little easier and more friendly to get into.

So make sure you design your site with the smallest files you can use and still get the job done.

- Use line drawings rather than glossy photographs.
- Don't bother with background music or video files.
- Put a small picture of your book cover (called a "thumbnail") with a link to the full-size version for those who want to see it and have the bandwidth to handle it.

Keep It Simple

The more difficult and complicated it is for visitors to find what they are looking for on your Web site, the less likely they'll take the time and trouble. As we said, you want to make sure that your first Web impression is a good one.

The best way to accomplish this is to make sure that your page downloads quickly, even for folks using a 56k modem, and that once it is downloaded, it is clean, simple, easy to understand and organized so visitors can find whatever they are looking for intuitively, with a minimum of effort.

The whole subject of designing for the Web has been studied exhaustively. Real experts in the field are highly regarded and even more highly paid. Luckily, a lot of these experts have written books about their art and craft or, better yet, have authored Web pages on the subject.

Here are several good books that forego the extremely technical in favor of clear, easy-to-understand techniques for the amateur and professional alike.

Books on Web Site Design

Don't Make Me Think! A Common Sense Approach to Web Usability, by Steve Krug and Roger Black, Que, 2000. In its review, Book News, Inc. said:

> Krug, a usability consultant who has worked for companies like Apple and Netscape, offers sharp observations, a healthy dash of humor, and straightforward solutions to fundamental Web design problems. He shows how to design pages for scanning, how to eliminate needless words, how to design a home page, and how to streamline design for user navigation. He also reveals why most Web design team arguments about usability are a waste of time, and tells how to avoid them.

Designing Web Usability: The Practice of Simplicity, by Jakob Nielsen, New Riders Publishing, 1999. On the Amazon.com Web site, Tom Peters, management expert, author (*In Search of Excellence, The Circle of Innovation*) had this to say about this book:

> Eighty gajillion things have been written about the Web. Do we need one more? Answer: Yes! If it's from Jakob Nielsen. *Designing Web Usability: The Practice of Simplicity* is a masterpiece. Jakob knows his stuff like, literally, no one else! This book is a pleasure to read. And invaluable. May simplicity rule!

Web Pages That Suck: Learn Good Design by Looking at Bad Design, by Vincent Flanders and Michael Willis, Sybex, 1988. Reviewing the book in *Dr. Dobb's Journal,* (www.ddj.com) John S. Rhodes said:

> In my opinion, Flanders and Willis were brave souls to trust that their offbeat style would successfully carry over to print. Yet, it is hard to deny that the approach works. I would even be roused to say that the book is superior and far more handy than the Web site. While they basically have the same content, the book is much more user-friendly. Accessing and understanding the information is easier because it is better organized. The bottom line is that the content of the book is excellent, and the authors' offbeat style makes the book enjoyable.

Web Site Design Help You Can Find Online

Web Sites That Suck.com: http://webpagesthatsuck.com. This is the Web site on which the book just mentioned is based. Here you can find examples of the winking and glaring and flashing type designs you *don't* want to use, especially if you want to keep your site simple. You can also find links here to articles by the authors, as well as other online Web design resources. We recommend this site highly, if only for the hilarious rant (with even more hilarious—and horrible—examples) against "Mystery Meat Navigation."

KrystalRose's Ten Commandments of Good Web Design (www.krystalrose.com/web/commandments.html). KrystalRose is a Web design firm that has formulated a simplified version of the basic principles of good Web design into the classic Ten Commandments format. Here's a sample:

1. Thou Shalt Not Make Thy Customers Wait Ten Minutes for Thy Page to Download. Graphics and whirly-gizmos are great. They can say more about you, in a few inches of browser real estate, than a thousand words. But if they are large, either physically or byte-wise, your customers are going to hit the "Back" button before they ever finish loading. The average Web surfer has an attention span of approximately seven seconds—if they don't see some information quickly, all the nifty effects in the world won't keep them on your page!

The Yale Web Style Guide (http://info.med.yale.edu/caim/manual/index.html), authored and maintained by Patrick J. Lynch and Sarah Horton, is a definite "don't miss." If you've progressed beyond the absolute basics of designing for the Web, you should probably check out this site. Lots and lots of information, as well as links to other excellent design resources.

Dr. Jakob Nielsen of the Nielsen Norman Group maintains an iconoclastic newsletter on the Alertbox Web site at www.useit.com/alertbox/. His site has dozens of previous columns archived—some with titles like "Why Frames Suck Most of the Time" and "How People Read on the Web." Dr. Nielsen is an internationally recognized expert on not only Web design, but also on how and why people make use of the Web. He is also the author of one of our recommended books, *Designing Web Usability: The Practice of*

Simplicity. Visit Dr. Nielsen's site at the Alertbox. We assure you, you won't regret it.

○ ○ ○

Between books and Web sites, there are numerous valuable resources where you can learn about making your Web site as useful and as attractive as possible.

CHAPTER TWENTY-SIX

REASONS FOR GIVING YOUR E-BOOK AWAY FOR FREE

The traditional model of print publishing, distribution and marketing was designed with one goal in mind: that each level of the system would have a chance to make a financial profit. Without profit, the entire system collapses because each level of the system costs somebody money. The publisher has to pay editors, printers, warehouse people and the guy who hauls out the trash.

One of the major factors bearing on your own publishing decisions will be of the most basic sort: Do you want to sell your book, or do you want to give it away?

Believe it or not, there are strong arguments for the free approach, even if your ultimate goal is to get paid for your writing. Writers have long complained that the seemingly rigid commercial requirements of big print publishers, with their emphasis on market niches, genres and categories, have prevented their work from even being considered for publication. And there may be some validity to these complaints: Print publishing exists on shaky financial underpinnings at the moment, and publishers have to consider the bottom line before they make the substantial investment involved in publishing a book. It is entirely possible that many otherwise worthy offerings slip through these financial cracks. Once upon a time that meant, for all intents and purposes, the end of the writer's options for publication. Thanks to the digital revolution, that is no longer the case.

Giving Your Work Away

Why would authors want to give their work away? Isn't that counterintuitive? Or at least counterproductive?

Not necessarily. For some authors, the knowledge that their work, on which they've spent so much time and effort, is being read by others provides all the satisfaction they need. For such writers, digital publication seems heaven-sent: Their potential audience is the millions of readers in the digital world.

And there is potential to turn your giveaway into something more substantial, career-wise. It is possible that you might manage to parlay good reviews and word-of-mouth "buzz" you receive after self-publishing your books for free on your Web sites into publishing contracts from the very houses that turned you down before.

If making a profit isn't your goal, then you need pay little mind to comparisons between digital and traditional publishing. You may have some other goals in mind that could, in some ways, be considered a form of profit, but you needn't worry about all the varied systems that have been developed to get cash into your own pocket.

All you need to know is the basic model of free e-publishing:

- Create a Web site.
- Render your e-books into as many formats as you desire.
- Place links to your e-books on your Web site.
- Publicize and market your Web site and the e-books on it.

That's it. You are now an e-publisher.

However, even if selling your work online is not your immediate goal, and all you seek is visibility and readers, you must still think in terms of marketing, because the simple truth is that there is considerable competition out there even for the free stuff.

CHAPTER TWENTY-SEVEN

HOW TO MAKE MONEY FROM YOUR E-BOOK

The world of e-publishing for profit is still in flux, but already several models have achieved some sort of currency. One of the original notions was the "advertising model." There are also "pay-per-view" and "pay-for-download" systems. A relatively new wrinkle is the "donation model." Another notion now beginning to garner a fair amount of interest is the "subscription" model. In the case of certain hybrid e-book–print book situations, there is the mail order model. Last, but certainly not least, is the traditional mainstream publishing model as adapted to electronic distribution.

PROFIT-MAKING MODELS

- Advertising
- Pay-per-view
- Pay-per-download
- Donation
- Traditional adapted for digital technology

Let's discuss each payment system, keeping in mind that the goal of all of them is to somehow provide a mechanism tailored specifically to the e-book that allows you, the publisher of an e-book, to get paid for publishing that book.

The Advertising Model

Entire dot.com empires were built on this model. As recently as 1998, it was generally considered to be the most obvious, efficient and lucrative way for people who provided "content" (including articles, jokes, commentary, instruction manuals, search engines and, yes, e-books) and, in some cases, services and even goods, to make a whole lot of money on the World Wide Web.

It works like this: You build a Web site and give Web surfers some compelling reason to visit. That reason might be a search engine like Yahoo! It might be an Internet magazine like Salon.com. It might be a page of links to various news stories and selected columnists, like the Drudge Report. Or it might be that book you've written, which is so interesting, so compelling that the word has gone out to millions of Web surfers who then click over to your site to find out what all the buzz is about.

It doesn't matter what causes folks to visit these pages. The mere fact that they come is enough because the idea isn't to sell whatever it is that is on the pages, it is to *sell advertising to people who want to place their ads on your Web site.*

Now, there is nothing at all revolutionary about this concept. It has supported newspapers and magazines for more than a hundred years.

Nor is there anything revolutionary about the notion of advertising-supported electronic media. Prior to the advent of cable television, the television networks were entirely supported by the commercials that viewers saw as they watched their favorite shows. The major television broadcasting networks are still completely supported this way, and the cable channels, while receiving part of their incomes from the monthly cable fees the viewer pays, are also supported to a large extent by commercial advertising revenues.

In other words, the advertising model has a long, proven history. Magazine and newspaper publishers understand it, as do the advertisers who make use of it. The basic relationship of such advertiser-supported models is also easily comprehended. The advertiser says: "The more people of the type I am looking for that you can guarantee will see my advertising, the more I am willing to pay you for it."

Into this well-understood and well-accepted model came the World Wide Web. According to "The Inside Scoop: Content Sites Will Work on the Web," by Christopher M. Schroeder, published in the *Wall Street Journal* on April 16, 2001, "Think about the advertising dollars that TV and cable attract. Then think about the fact that the Internet surpassed 50 million users in less than five years, while it took radio, TV and cable 38, 13 and 10 years respectively to get there. Ponder the fact that 35 million U.S. households are set to have Internet access this year, and that over two-thirds of online households make regular purchases on the Internet, while half research online before buying offline. And consider that, despite incredible recent growth, wireless and broadband are only in their infancy."

Those are pretty impressive numbers. And they were impressive back in the late nineties when similar numbers helped to drive the incredible Internet boom that saw companies that had once lost money at amazing rates suddenly achieve stock valuations of hundreds of dollars per share.

Everybody believed that this advertising-supported model would support the World Wide Web and, even more, make the Web the richest, most revolutionary gold mine in financial history.

Except it didn't happen—not permanently, at least. Over a period of two or three years, almost everybody associated with the Web in any way made money. Then it stopped. Hundreds of commercial, advertiser-supported Web sites went out of business.

What happened? How could the advertising-supported model, which had been so effective, so trustworthy, for so many years, result in such a tremendous failure?

The answer is simple: The Internet and the World Wide Web really are revolutionary. So revolutionary that nobody really knew how to quantify all those people who were using it. Netheads called people viewing Web pages "eyeballs." If a surfer looked at one page, that was an eyeball. Some Web sites garnered millions, even hundreds of millions, of eyeballs a month. Developers took these eyeball figures to the advertisers and created advertising rates based on eyeballs. Only one problem: There didn't seem to be any correlation between eyeballs and actual sales of the product advertised.

And there still doesn't seem to be. When advertisers put up hard cash, they expect a return. They expect to see sales go up in the demographic areas they target. Magazine, newspaper and television advertising have been measuring the relationship between their version of eyeballs and the sales resulting from those eyeballs for decades now. Advertisers can safely predict, within a few decimal points, how much their advertising dollar will affect sales in any of these older mediums.

Advertisers suddenly couldn't see any "bang for their buck" to advertising on the Web, and so they cut way back. The problem was further compounded by the fact that a large percentage of Internet advertising was coming from other Internet companies, who were also trying to develop income streams from advertising. Eventually, the whole house of cards collapsed.

And what about you? Should you try to get your money by e-publishing your book on your own Web site and then seeking advertisers?

The answer is as old as print books themselves. How many ads do you see in the print books you buy? Not many, right? There are several reasons for this: First, people don't seem to *like* having their books interrupted by ads. Second, the number of people who read books, while reasonably large, pales in comparison to the number of people who read magazines and newspapers or watch television.

"Wait a minute!" you reply. "I'm not going to put ads in my e-books—just on my Web site." Well, unfortunately, the same metrics apply. In order to make your site attractive to advertisers, you would somehow have to show them millions of eyeballs, and even then, they'd have to be the right kind of eyeballs. If you are promoting your gripping novels of wartime derring-do, chances are your site would be of small interest to advertisers hoping to reach the 15–25 female market.

We could go on, but the bottom line is this: You are probably not going to be able to earn large amounts through advertising on your Web site.

However, the possibility of earning a small income does exist. You can look into "associate programs," which quite a few merchants have developed to support their own products. These work on a "click-through and sell" basis. Once you join a program, you place a small ad or just a link for the advertiser's product on your Web site. If a surfer clicks on the link (which takes them to a page designed by the merchant) and then *buys the merchant's product,* you will receive a payment based on your agreement with that advertiser.

For an excellent overview of the world of associate advertising programs, visit the iBoost.com Web site at www.iboost.com/profit/advertising/articles/06018.htm.

Pay-Per-View

This is exactly what it sounds like. You post your e-book on your Web site. Folks go to your site and, before they can access your book, they have to pay. A variation is to allow the surfer to read some part of your book—perhaps the first chapter—and then charge him to view the rest of the book.

We won't spend much time on this because it doesn't work. No person with any Web savvy at all will pay merely to view e-book content on a Web site. At the very least, they must be able to download the e-book file to their own computer.

Why, you might wonder, would we mention two models that don't work or don't work very well? Because the Web changes constantly. What didn't work yesterday may work perfectly well tomorrow. Recently, some experts like James Cramer, an investor in the subscription financial Web site RealMoney.com, are making the case for advertising support for Web sites again. Cramer points out that certain types of Web sites draw a highly marketable type of user and that advertisers should be willing to pay to establish a presence on such sites simply as a form of product awareness. He notes that in no other form of advertising do advertisers demand the rigid, one-to-one results between page views and sales that they demanded of Web advertising. Cramer may well be right. At this point, his is a minority view. A few years from now, his opinion may become ironclad reality.

The Donation Model

This one is interesting. It is a sort of cross between free distribution and for-pay distribution. We suspect that there are many self-e-publishers (those who publish only their own e-books) who may find this method quite useful.

In a nutshell, you set up your e-publishing Web site to allow your readers to download your work without cost. If they choose to do so, that is the end of the matter. However, you also set up on your site a method by which readers, if they desire, can donate a small sum to you to express their satisfaction with your offerings.

The logic behind the donation model satisfies one of the controversies currently abroad in the world of e-publishing—the conflict between those who believe that all information should be freely exchanged and those who believe that writers should be paid for their work if they so desire. The donation model lets the customer resolve the question by not forcing payment, but allowing for it. In this way, intellectual property is freely distributed, but a mechanism exists to allow payment. Even more revolutionary, the customer is allowed to set the payment, rather than being forced to pay some set cover price. There is a weird kind of logic to this: Most folks have read books they thought were worth far more to them than what they paid. They've also read books they thought were much overpriced for the value they received. The donation model provides a way to resolve all these controversies in one simple step.

A seemingly natural fit for e-publishers might be the honor system, a donation/payment system set up by the huge online bookseller Amazon.com. The reason for the good fit is that the twenty-nine million folks already signed up at Amazon can use the system without doing anything beyond clicking on an icon on your Web page—and those millions are signed up at Amazon because they are interested in books. If they buy books at Amazon, they are already accustomed to buying books on the Web, so perhaps they will also be interested in giving you a donation for the pleasure they get from reading your e-books.

The Amazon honor system has some limits: The minimum donation allowed is $1, the maximum $50. And Amazon, as a protection against fraud, sets limits on the total amount of donations you can receive, although these limits are negotiable, depending on your circumstances.

The system is based on the donor having a credit card from which these small payments are deducted. Folks without credit cards (Are there any of those left?) will be unable to donate through the honor system. At present, the system charges you, the recipient, 15 cents per transaction, plus 15 percent of the amount of the transaction. In the case of a donation of $1, this would mean you would net 70 cents, although a donation of $5 would put $4 in your pocket.

A Donor Success Story

If you'd like to see how the donor system can work successfully, the well-known writer Andrew Sullivan uses it to accept donations at his Web site, www.andrewsullivan.com. Sullivan added a small icon to his main Web page that the donor can click on and go directly to a donation page. He also periodically mentions on his site that he accepts donations and posts an occasional total of the amount he has received and how he plans to use the income to improve his Web site.

You can find out how to set up Amazon.com's honor system on your own Web site by going to http://s1.amazon.com/exec/varzea/ subst/fx/home.html/102-9626660-5263365. The process is relatively simple and can be done on the Web site itself. Just follow the directions you find there.

This is the only system we know of right now that's set up to permit donations to a Web site. We think it is worthwhile.

The Subscription Model

This method of earning money is another oldie but goodie. Magazines, newspapers and cable television use it. You pay a certain amount per month or year and have access to all the content available in the distribution channel. In your case, the distribution channel is your Web site, and the content is your e-book.

But you have to ask yourself whether this model is, at this point, well adapted to the process of selling e-books on the Web. With the recent collapse of the advertising model, many Web sites are turning to a subscription model as a source of revenue. And while subscriptions may be feasible for well-established Web sites that offer a constant stream of fresh content—like newsmagazines or business commentary sites—we don't think this notion will work very well if your intention is to sell an e-book title or two. However, if you are prolific enough to give your readers a reason to return again and again, you might consider it. You might even consider setting up a part of your Web site for a regularly updated series of columns or essays of general interest to your potential e-book customers in order to bring them back on a continuing basis.

Certain nonfiction subjects that can be frequently updated work better for this method. For example, if your e-book is on collecting antiques, a constantly updated pricing guide could give your readers a reason to keep coming back to your site.

If you decide to use this model, you need to set up a method of payment and then password-protect either the part of your Web site where the e-books can be downloaded or the e-books themselves.

Password-protecting Web pages—making them viewable only by supplying a password—by using the free capabilities built into most Web servers is a technical subject: If you're looking for a reasonably clear explanation, see the discussion of htpasswd at http://home.crosslink.net/webhelp/protect.html.

If you'd rather avoid the technical stuff entirely, you'll want to spend $24.95 to buy a neat little program called HTMlock, which lets you create passwords for any Web page on your Web site with only a few mouseclicks. Made by VirTime, this program is available at www.virtime.com/htl/.

Pay-Per-Download

The pay-per-download is the model that we think most self-e-publishers will use. It is simple in concept and analogous to the way people are already accustomed to buying books: go to the bookstore (in your case, your Web site), select the books they want, pay for them and take them home.

The general principle is the same as for the free e-publishing site, with one addition: You need to provide a mechanism to pay for the books.

Unless you have a large number of e-books for sale, the easiest way to accept payment is to use a service that already exists to do the work for you.

One of the most widely known payment services is PayPal (www .paypal.com). PayPal allows folks to use credit cards or direct transfers from their checking accounts to send money to you. You don't need to have a merchant credit card account in order to accept payment, and if your customers have a checking account, they don't need to have a credit card to pay you. PayPal also offers a variation of their service called "Web Accept," which is specifically tailored to online e-commerce. Go to www.paypal.com/cgi-bin/webscr?cm d = p/web/index-outside to see the simple instructions.

Another possibility is to use the Amazon honor system, which we previously discussed. The honor system offers an alternative that allows a direct payment rather than a donation, although the same fees apply.

Either of these systems will serve you well if you have just a few e-books you wish to sell, and you don't have to be a technical genius to figure out how to use them.

Making a Profit Is Within Your Reach

We've spent a considerable amount of time to get to this point. Some of the concepts we've discussed may seem technical or difficult for you folks who don't think of yourself as Web wizards. But the basic idea of self-e-publishing is simple, and implementing it is within the reach of most people. Millions of people have already managed to use each of the payment methods we discussed. You can, too, and we assure you, you will.

CHAPTER TWENTY-EIGHT

CONGRATULATIONS! YOU ARE AN E-BOOK PUBLISHER

We've explained how to set up a basic "Storefront on the Web" from which you can make your books available to the world. Now you should know that you don't need to be the General Electric of Web sites. All you need is a clean and comfortable place where readers can easily obtain your books. There are hundreds of millions of Web pages out there, most of them designed and created by folks just like you. So don't be baffled or buffaloed by the process, just dive right in. You can get it done.

Once you have your Web "publishing house" set up, look back to the chapters in section two on formatting, to make sure you have your books formatted in such a way that the majority of your readers can read them. Once you've gotten to this point, you've pretty much completed the basic requirements of e-publishing.

Take a deep breath. Don't you feel great? You should, you know—because you've now accomplished all the steps you need to call yourself an e-publisher. You have *prepared and issued material for public distribution or sale.*

And you've done it all by yourself. If the "power of the press is reserved for those who own one," you are, thanks to the revolution of digital publishing, as powerful as any of the great print publishers—

**STEPHEN KING: THE MOST SUCCESSFUL
SELF-E-PUBLISHER IN HISTORY**

King's serial novel, *The Plant*, and his novelette, *Riding the Bullet*, have sold hundreds of thousands of copies in e-book formats on the Web, far more than any other such efforts.

maybe even more so because your potential reach—and markets— are greater than any that have ever existed before.

So give yourself a pat on the back. For some of you, you've learned everything you need. You've e-published your e-book. For others, though, especially those of you who want a wide readership or hope to achieve a significant number of sales of your work, there is more. Grab a fresh cup of coffee, stretch a bit and then come back to find out what.

PART FOUR

Working With Others to E-Publish Your E-Book

CHAPTER TWENTY-NINE

HOW BRAND-NAME E-PUBLISHERS CAN HELP YOUR CAREER

U p to now, we've concentrated on a kind of "do-it-yourself" version of e-publishing. But what if, no matter how simple and easy the process is, this sort of thing just isn't your cup of tea? Are you and your books doomed to be locked out of the digital revolution forever?

Not at all.

In fact, a thriving industry has sprung up to address the needs of those of you who don't want to "do it yourself." Amazingly enough, this industry bears a strong resemblance to the print publishing business that has existed for hundreds of years.

Print publishers, with their vast stores of backlisted titles and their ability to field large marketing and public relations budgets, have been relatively slow to exploit the promise of e-publishing. There's a good reason for this: They have so much at stake, they have a great deal to lose if they make mistakes. Their natural tendency is to move slowly. After all, the sales of print books dwarf the sales of the e-publishing industry on a huge scale.

But the print publishing model is a different story. Most writers are familiar with this model: You find (or try very hard to find) an agent to represent you. The agent sends your manuscript to editors at print publishing houses. If an editor likes your book and thinks her employers can make a profit by publishing it, the house offers you a publishing contract, which most likely includes provisions for an advance payment and royalty payments on sales further down the road.

The editor then works with you to make any changes she feels are necessary to improve the prospects of the book. The final draft is checked by a copy editor. A book cover is ordered. If you are lucky, a marketing budget for the book is also approved, and advertising, even a book tour, are arranged. The book is printed and shipped to bookstores, and you become an officially published, in-print author.

The differences between this process and the self-e-publishing process we've so far concentrated on are obvious. As a self-e-publisher, you don't need to look for an agent or a publisher—you are your own publisher. You don't sign any contracts. The only editors you work with are ones you hire. And you handle all the distribution and marketing of your book through your Web bookstore.

But what if you don't want to do all that nonwriting work? You'd rather have someone else do it, just like the print publishing houses do. So, are there such things as e-publishing houses?

Yes, of course there are. In fact, there are dozens of them. They operate very similarly to print publishers, except that they make use of the Internet and the digital revolution to distribute e-books. Otherwise, their publishing process mimics that of print publishing almost every step of the way. You query them, and they choose to either publish you or not publish you depending on the quality and appropriateness of your work.

In addition, some of the print publishing houses have actually gone so far as to create online e-publishing subsidiaries: atRandom, www.randomhouse.com/atrandom/, a subsidiary of the well-known Random House, is one example. But for every traditional publisher making a move into the new world of e-publishing, we can easily find ten, or even a hundred, electronic publishing houses created specifically to exploit the new powers and capabilities of the digital revolution. One of them may be just the place for you.

First, let's consider the advantages of such venues for the author. As we've noted, these e-publishers relieve the writer (at least, most of them do) of the necessity of dealing with the digital nuts and bolts of e-publishing. E-publishers have their own Web sites, so you don't need one. They will handle designing a cover for your book. They will often provide your book with an editor. And, perhaps most important, they offer the writer the advantages of what we call a *branded* "gateway" or "portal."

Now what does this mean? In this sense, we use "branded" to mean a place whose "name" or "brand" is, to some extent, at least, well known. Further, what is generally known about this "name brand" is reassuring to the consumer.

For instance, let's take a look at Amazon.com, one of the most successful dot.coms at establishing a brand name. Through dint of good Web design, excellent support systems and the expenditure of huge amounts of money, Amazon.com has managed, in a few short years, to make its name one of the best known in the world. For most folks who plan to buy books on the Internet, the first place they think of to shop is Amazon.com, the "world's biggest bookstore," as Amazonians like to put it.

Further, because of their vast selection, customer security features and rapid order fulfillment, when most people think of Amazon, they are reassured that this is a good place to buy books online. That is good branding has been of enormous help to Amazon.com and one of the main reasons its operations have grown with amazing rapidity.

Barnes & Noble (www.bn.com) is one of Amazon.com's principle online competitors (and, unlike Amazon.com, it has hundreds of real-world "brick-and-mortar" bookstores as well). The other large chain bookstore, Borders, works with Amazon to sell books online. Both of these huge booksellers have highly efficient, highly visible presences on the Web, and you most certainly want them to carry your books as well.

How Brand-Name E-Publishers Can Help Your Career

Many print publishing houses have managed, over the years, to enjoy similar success in establishing their own brands. A major reason for this is that print houses are set up to function not just as well-known purveyors of books but as *quality filters* for the books they market.

Most readers understand that by the time a print book has made it through the print publishing process, it will meet some minimum but generally acceptable standard of quality. The text will be properly copyedited. The mere fact that the publisher has paid its own cash to the author also means that the publisher expects—well, hopes—to make a profit on the book, usually because people have bought sufficient numbers of similar books in the past. This indicates that some readers, at least, will find the book attractive and satisfying.

All of these notions are washing around in the subconscious of book buyers as they browse the shelves of their favorite bookstores, barely noticing the insignia of the various publishing houses on the spine of the books, but comforted, nonetheless, by the knowledge that those same houses have given them reading pleasure in the past.

Another form of branding is, of course, the names of well-known authors themselves. Stephen King could probably publish his latest horror-rama on unbound tissue paper and distribute it from a sidewalk packing crate in Poughkeepsie, and his legions of fans would still line up to buy because they know and like what they will get from him. He has become a brand unto himself, independent of any publisher's brand, which is probably a major reason why his ventures into e-publishing have been so successful.

Like the well-established houses and authors, e-publishing houses hope to establish the same kind of brand awareness that mainstream print publishers already enjoy. Those that are successful at branding offer the author of electronic books the same publishing experience as print publishers, which we will discuss in the following chapter.

CHAPTER THIRTY

WORKING WITH ESTABLISHED E-PUBLISHERS

Many of the established print publishers, as we've noted, are now beginning very slowly to move into the world of e-publishing. We cited atRandom, Random House's e-publishing venture, as an example. But there are many more publishers who exist entirely on the Web and use the Internet as their sole marketing, distribution and sales tool.

If any of these Web publishers were to develop the same level of customer trust that the print houses have built up over the years, they might offer a much more powerful outlet for your work than you can achieve by simply putting up your own page on the Web and hoping for the best.

But do they?

The jury is still out. Let's take a look at the usual publication process used by these Web publishing operations and how it compares and contrasts with the print publishers, with an eye to discovering whether they do offer brands as powerful as the longer-established traditional publishers.

First, keep in mind that the print houses buy much less than 1 percent of all unsolicited manuscripts they receive—estimates run as low as 0.1 percent. Obviously, from a writer's perspective, this can be either a good or bad practice. If you're one of the lucky and talented 0.1 percent, it probably looks good. But if you fall into the remaining 99.9, you will probably view this system with frustration.

Nevertheless, this extreme selectivity on the part of print publishers is the first, and perhaps most major, step in establishing a *quality filter*. Now, we won't try to convince you that the 0.1 percent is selected solely on pure literary merit. After all, publishers—and this definitely includes e-publishers—are looking for books they can sell in a sufficient number to make a profit. Given that public tastes can sometimes incline in the direction of books that could in no way be considered literary masterpieces, we'd be foolish to tell you that profit potential does not on occasion outweigh pure literary merit.

That said, print publishers reject the vast majority of books on issues of basic quality. Manuscripts littered with misspellings, bad grammar and punctuation, or an obvious lack of writing skill or professional-level know-how are quickly discarded.

Here is how one editor, writing for the Web site *The Writer's Home Companion* in an article titled "A Spin in the Editor's Chair" (www.writershome.com/instruction/presenting.htm#spin), described the slush-pile process:

> First, without even opening them, I can discard the letters that come in small envelopes: too much unfolding, if they are not written on notepaper. If they are, I'm not interested anyway, because undersize sheets get lost in my standard 8½″ × 11″ files. Next, I can discard all those addressed to an editor who died over a year ago and those addressed to me but misspelling my name.
>
> Ah, here are three that had postage due, one more in a bright red envelope, two that smell of perfume, and one that says, 'You're gonna love this' on the outside. They can go. Mmmm, four written in pencil, one with an ink smudge, and two from the same guy, both addressed to an editor for an-

other magazine. As the day wears on, others are discarded because they are typed with a pale ribbon, written in longhand or typed in script. Several go right to the shredder because they are not accompanied by SASEs (self-addressed stamped envelopes).

Pretty tough. But this winnowing of the slush pile does guarantee that a great deal of bad writing, or at least nonprofessional writing, never makes it onto the bookshelves or into a dissatisfied reader's hands.

Books accepted for publication by print publishers go through a well-defined process of editing and copyediting designed to improve the work as much as possible (the definition of "improve" is determined in general by the judgments of the publisher and its editors) and eliminate those glitches that slip by even the best of writers. In the end, individual readers may disagree as to the quality of the final product, but in fact most books published by print houses do sell at least a few thousand copies. Somebody out there likes them.

E-Publishers Vs. Print Publishers

How well do the online Web publishers function at the same game? Well, if the truth be told, performance can be spotty. Some places we visited offered works indistinguishable in quality from those found in print bookstores, and, in fact, were written by e-publishing authors who had impressive strings of credits in print publishing.

Others, however, had published works that we can most charitably describe only as marginal. How can you, as a writer interested in making use of branded e-publishing houses, tell the difference?

The best way is simply to go look. Most of these e-publishers allow you to read samples from each book they publish. Put on your reader hat and do so. As you read, ask yourself if what you

WHERE TO FIND ONLINE LISTS OF E-PUBLISHERS

If working with an established e-publisher sounds like the route you want to take, you're probably wondering how you find these e-publishers. Here are several online resources that list and comment on e-publishers. Check out the e-publisher's site for specific information on what to send when you are submitting your manuscript for consideration.

- **eBooks-n-Bytes:** (www.ebooksnbytes.com/epub_list.html) maintains a large list of e-publishers, along with a thumbnail write-up on each house. The write-ups offer concise, worthwhile information.
- **eBook Palace:** (www.ebooksearchengine.com/cgi-bin/ebooks/eboo ks.cgi?search-CAT&category-Ebook%20Publishers lists thirty-nine e-publishers with links and brief commentary. An added twist: The number of visits from eBook Palace's Web site to each e-publisher's Web site is noted.
- **Writers Write:** (www.writerswrite.com/epublishing/epublishers .htm) maintains a list of e-book publishers, as well as a wide selection of links to other lists and data about e-publishing.
- **Crowsnest Books:** (www.computercrowsnest.com/greennebula/ dir_publishers.htm) offers a good selection of links to many e-publishers.
- **Association of Electronic Publishers:** a trade group, maintains listings of its members at http://members.tripod.com/~BestBooks Com/AEP/aepmembers.html. In order to join the AEP, members must meet stringent requirements that limit membership to e-publishers who can demonstrate legitimacy as ongoing publishing operations. This is not to say that nonmembers are not legitimate, only that AEP members have met certain standards of association approval.

An excellent print resource of e-publisher listings is *Writer's Online Marketplace* by Debbie Ridpath Ohi. And remember, it is a good idea to check out the quality of an e-publisher's Web site and book selections before you send them your manuscript.

are reading reaches a level of quality you would pay money for if you found it in a print bookstore. If it does, all e-publishers have instructions on their Web sites as to the proper method of submitting your manuscript for their consideration.

If the work you read does not meet what you consider to be reasonable standards of quality, then ask yourself if you want your work to be associated with the books you've just read.

Remember: Just like anyone else, authors are known by the company they and their books keep.

CHAPTER THIRTY-ONE

IS A VANITY E-PUBLISHER RIGHT FOR YOU?

There is one other form of Internet publishing that has existed in the print world for a long time and has quickly made the jump to the digital world as well. *Vanity publishers* are "publishing" operations which offer, or claim to offer, all of the services a standard royalty publisher performs; the only difference is that the author bears the costs for the printing and marketing, rather than the publisher.

Now, if what you are looking for is somebody else to do the work, and you are willing to pay them to do it, then a legitimate vanity publisher may meet your needs perfectly. The key word here is "legitimate." There are hundreds, perhaps thousands, of Web sites where various publishing operations offer to turn your written manuscript into a digital book and distribute that book either in electronic format, as print on demand, even in hardcover. They will also create cover and internal artwork, provide editing services, in fact do what any standard publisher would do—all for a fee.

Some of these operations charge for anything and everything they do, right down to postage stamps and interoffice memos on an individual basis. Others offer "packages" of services at varying levels of cost. The more expensive the package, the more services included.

Does this sound like something you think you might be interested in? If so, allow us to offer a few caveats.

First, especially in the realm of e-publishing, there is very little a vanity publisher can do for you that you can't do for yourself. You'll see many such operations make wild, expansive claims on their Web sites, particularly in the area of marketing. They'll say they will put your book "on every major Internet search engine." Well, you can do the same with a few mouse clicks, and we'll tell you how in the chapters on marketing. They'll "build and maintain a Web site for your book." We've already explained how you can do that for yourself, quickly, easily, and most important, cheaply. And they will assure you that your book will be intensively marketed from their Web site. Quick! Name the e-publishing vanity house that springs to mind as soon as you think about the subject of self-publishing.

Can't think of any? We aren't surprised. We couldn't, either.

One more thing to consider: Vanity publishers don't act as a "quality filter" at all. The only thing they filter is the ability of the writer to pay them. Anybody who can afford the fees can be "published" by one of these operations. Because of this, not only do many authors and readers tend to mistrust the quality of such publishing efforts, many distribution channels, including wholesalers, bookstores and online bookstores refuse to stock books published in this way.

Still, despite these caveats, you might wish to persevere. Reasons for doing so could include your desire to take advantage of a vanity e-publisher's ability to publish your work as a print-on-demand book. This would be particularly true for authors who have written "proprietary" works like family genealogies or histories or esoteric scientific treatises of little or no interest to the general reading public. Authors of such works might well need a way for a small group to obtain printed copies of the work.

Which brings us to our original contention: How can you tell if a Web-based vanity publisher is legitimate? By legitimate, we mean they will deliver quality work for the payment they charge.

Author Victoria Strauss, at her Science Fiction and Fantasy Writers of America Web site Writers Beware! (www.sfwa.org/bew are/) has an extensive menu of links about many of the pitfalls of publishing, both online and off.

In an article on the subject at www.sfwa.org/beware/subsidypubl ishers.html, Strauss addresses many of the issues we've touched upon. Here are some excerpts from that article:

SUBSIDY AND VANITY PUBLISHERS

Victoria Strauss

Royalty publishers, subsidy publishers, vanity presses, self-publishing—what's the difference?

A royalty publisher purchases a manuscript as a property and pays the author a royalty on sales (most also pay an advance on royalties). Royalty publishers handle every aspect of publication, distribution, and marketing. There are no costs to the author.

A vanity publisher prints and binds a book at the author's sole expense. The completed books are the property of the author, and the author retains all proceeds from sales. Vanity publishers provide no editing, marketing, warehousing, or promotional services.

A subsidy publisher (also called a joint venture or co-op publisher) also takes payment from the author to print and bind a book, but may itself contribute a portion of the cost. In addition, a subsidy publisher may provide other services, including editing, distribution, warehousing, and marketing. As with a royalty publisher, the completed books are the property of the publisher, and remain in the publisher's possession until sold. Income to the writer comes in the form of a royalty.

Self-publishing, like vanity publishing, requires the author to undertake the entire cost of publication him/herself, and to handle all marketing, distribution, storage, etc. However, because the author can put every aspect of the process out to bid, rather than accepting a pre-set package of services, self-publishing can be more cost-effective than vanity or subsidy publishing, and can result in a much higher-quality product. And unlike subsidy publishing, the completed books are the property of the writer, which means that the writer keeps 100 percent of the proceeds from sales.

Look at other books the publisher has produced to ascertain quality. Have the books been proofread? Are all the pages in order? Is the cover art attractive? In other words, do the books produce a professional impression?

Request references. And use them.

Seek out and talk to other people who've used the publisher's services (not necessarily the people the publisher has given as references). Are they happy with the quality of the books? Did they receive all the books they paid for? Did they have any problems getting hold of their books after they were published? Have there been any broken promises?

Strauss continues with several other common-sense admonishments, advising would-be self-publishers to verify any promises made to them beforehand; for instance, if a marketing program is offered, be sure to ask for samples of brochures, ads, publicity releases and such.

There are other warning signs authors should be aware of. A referral to a subsidy publisher from an agent or a freelance editor is one of them. (Reputable agents and editors don't work with subsidy publishers, Strauss says.) A stated or implied promise of a profit on a book project. Most telling of all, obfuscation or flat refusal on the part of the publisher when the author makes reasonable requests for information, especially a refusal to supply a firm price quotation before the contract is signed.

Something else to watch out for are verbal promises that are not mirrored in the contract. Remember, the only thing binding on either party is the contents of the contract itself. As famous movie producer Samuel Goldwyn once said, "Verbal contracts aren't worth the paper they're printed on."

Strauss mentions other red flags:

- Extravagant praise or promises.
- A contract that doesn't require you to pay for publication, but does require you to pay for something else, like purchasing a specific number of books.
- Double standards that say since you aren't a published author, the publisher can only offer you a "co-op" deal, with you picking up "part" of the cost. All too often, the part you pick up is all of the cost.
- Publishers that portray themselves as standard small presses and don't reveal that the writer must pay a vanity fee until well into the "publishing" process.
- Pressure. Here Strauss refers to basic high-pressure sales tactics such as statements that the "offer" is good for a "limited time only" or that "costs will be going up soon."

If, after reading this information on vanity e-publishers, you still want to pay one to create and distribute your e-book, go right ahead. But don't say we—and Victoria Strauss—didn't warn you.

CHAPTER THIRTY-TWO

WORKING WITH PRINT-ON-DEMAND PUBLISHERS

As we've noted, the ability to print books on demand is a hybrid process that combines elements of both print and electronic publishing. POD books don't exist in tangible form until one is ordered and printed, thus eliminating inventory and storage costs, as well as the built-in wastage of the old-style returns system. On the other hand, after they are printed, POD books are identical to print books in every way because they *are* print books.

Some observers feel that POD is the transitional technology that will carry both standard and e-publishers, as well as readers, over the "digital hump" into tomorrow's all-digital publishing world.

It's probably too early to make that call. However, it doesn't take great intelligence to see that POD books can offer an interesting and potentially valuable new option to those who wish to take advantage of the technology.

Let's say that someone is you. You've thought about it and decided you want to offer your work to readers in a printed format and POD looks like a good way to do it. Are there any issues about print on demand you should be aware of?

Yes. And Victoria Strauss has written an excellent article about them, maintained on the Science Fiction and Fantasy Writers of

America Web site at www.sfwa.org/beware/printondemand.html #Fee.

Be sure to read the entire article, but here are some excerpts that deal with many of the vexing questions about POD:

PRINT ON DEMAND

Victoria Strauss

Many POD services call themselves self-publishing services. Some will even let you put the name of your own imprint on your book. It should be noted, however, that there are important differences between self-publishing and fee-based POD:

- **Control:** With self-publishing, the writer controls *all aspects* of the publishing process, from cover art to print style to pricing. With fee-based POD, the only choice the writer has is the package of services the publisher offers.
- **Profit:** With self-publishing, the writer keeps *all proceeds* from his/her sales. With fee-based POD, payment comes in the form of a royalty.
- **Rights:** With self-publishing, *all rights* remain with the writer, who has complete ownership of his/her books. With fee-based POD, rights often go to the POD company, which has an exclusive claim on them for a set period of time.

In reality, fee-based POD companies more closely resemble vanity publishers—which is, in fact, how they're widely perceived by readers, reviewers, and booksellers.

Writers considering fee-based POD should also be aware that:

Booksellers are unwilling to stock—and sometimes to order—books from fee-based PODs. Fee-based PODs usually make their books available for order by bookstores through the catalogue of a major wholesaler such as Ingram. But "available" doesn't mean "stockable." Booksellers are accustomed to buying books at a standard discount, to 60- or 90-day billing, and to being able to return unsold books for full credit. But POD books can't be offered at the standard discount, because they're more expensive to produce; additionally, fee-based PODs require orders to be pre-paid, and won't accept returns. This trio of factors makes it unlikely that any bookseller will be willing to place a POD book on its shelves.

Additionally, booksellers' policies on ordering fee-based POD books vary. Some will order any book you ask for. Others are selective—Barnes & Noble, for instance, which owns a stake in fee-based POD company iUniverse, will only order iUniverse books. And I've been receiving reports that some booksellers refuse to carry POD books in their computer systems at all.

The upshot: Like an e-book, a fee-based POD book will likely be available only through online sources.

POD books can be more expensive than traditionally printed books. POD prices are based on the amount of paper it takes to print the book. If your book is more than about 250 pages, it will cost a lot—sometimes a whole lot—more than a book of equivalent length printed the traditional way. This can be a substantial discouragement for buyers.

Books from fee-based POD companies won't be reviewed in major venues. This isn't just because they're widely perceived as vanity-published, but because most major review venues, such as *Publishers Weekly*, *Booklist*, and *Library Journal*, will only review bound galleys in advance of publication. Fee-based POD companies don't issue these.

Delays are possible. No one seems to know quite why, but fee-based PODs are experiencing a logjam in book production and order fulfillment. Many writers report substantial delays—sometimes as much as 6–8 weeks for orders.

There may be extra expenses. The cost of fee-based PODs can be substantially increased by additional charges not included in the initial package: renewal fees, extra charges for cover design, extra charges for an editing or marketing package, charges for obtaining an ISBN number, copyright registration, etc. Some services that advertise themselves as free charge so much for extras that they're actually more expensive than services that only charge a setup fee. Others charge a high fee for things you can purchase on your own for much less, such as copyright registration.

Royalties may be less than you think. Fee-based PODs are likely to pay royalties not as a percentage of a book's selling price, but of its net price—the selling price less the publisher's overhead (often not specified, so you're not sure exactly what you're getting). Depending on the discount (booksellers such as Amazon.com buy at a discount of 55 percent), that 30 percent royalty may actually work out to only 15 percent.

Your contract may be nonstandard. In commercial print publishing, contracts vary in their particulars, but tend to share a basic boilerplate. With fee-based PODs, there's no standardization, and many take serious advantage of that. Fee-based POD contracts can be incomplete, exploitive, or even outright abusive. I've seen contracts that provided no termination clauses, made no provisions for reverting rights back to the author, had unacceptable indemnification clauses, took ownership of the author's work, assigned the publisher an irrevocable interest in the author's future work, failed to adequately define royalty payments, empowered the publisher to excerpt writers' work for its own compilations without further permission . . . the list goes on.

Other potential problems with print on demand: The author bears all the responsibility for marketing. A fee-based POD work won't be considered a professional credit by many readers, reviewers and publishing pros, since they regard it as essentially the same thing as vanity publishing.

Your sales will most likely be low. Strauss notes that Xlibris, one of the largest fee-based POD companies, reports that its best-selling title so far has only racked up sales of between one and two thousand copies.

We don't want to sound unnecessarily gloomy about your prospects of finding legitimate e-publishing and print-on-demand operations. However, we do want you to be aware of some of the potential pitfalls, and we want you to arm yourself with the knowledge that will enable you to tell the difference between the good and the bad, as you would no doubt try to do with any other important consumer decision.

CHAPTER THIRTY-THREE

WRITER BEWARE: SCAMS IN ELECTRONIC PUBLISHING

For some reason, writers seem particularly susceptible to scams aimed at them, particularly scams involving agents, publishing and editing "services." Some practices, like the one involving Edit, Ink (read the full, awful tale here: www.sfwa.org/beware/Editink.html), became Net legends. Similar companies are operating today.

In cases such as these, knowledge is your best protection. We've found a few other excellent sites that will tell you what you need to know in order to protect yourself.

- **Preditors and Editors:** David Kuzminski's Preditors and Editors (www.sfwa.org/prededitors) is one of the most useful sites on the Web for those who want to be able to separate the honest wheat from the fraudulent chaff. P&E maintains up-to-date lists of agents, publishers and other firms of interest to writers, along with a rating system that includes both recommendations and non-recommendations. They post the reasons for their judgments as well, so you can make up your own mind. Highly recommended.

- **National Writers Union Alerts Page:** The National Writers Union maintains a page of alerts about various scams reported to them by their members at www.nwu.org/alerts/alrthome.htm.

While not as complete or as thorough as the preditors and editors site, it is worth a visit.

- **The Writer's Center:** The Writer's Center at www.writer.org/ scamkit.htm offers a "scam kit," a collection of rules and tests that lets the writer make decisions about the trustworthiness of various writing and publishing offerings. An explanatory article by Allan Lefcowitz, the artistic director of The Writer's Center, is provided at the Web address above as well as links to more materials.

○ ○ ○

Using the resources available on any of these sites, you will be better prepared to make informed decisions about e-publishers and agents.

CHAPTER THIRTY-FOUR

THE TRADITIONAL ROLE OF AGENTS

As you are considering the various methods you can take to get your e-book published, you may be wondering whether or not you need an agent in order to get published on the Web or through print on demand. To help answer this question, consider for a minute how agents came to their position of power in the first place.

Several years ago, the famous national magazine *The Saturday Evening Post* did an analysis of the history of their slush pile. Remember, the slush pile is what print editors call those piles of unsolicited manuscripts they receive from aspiring writers every day. Over the years, the *Post* had received hundreds of thousands of such manuscripts, all of which were at least opened and glanced at by readers and editors.

The magazine was interested in determining how many stories it had actually purchased from its slush pile. When the final results were in, the editors were astonished. They discovered that the magazine had bought less than half a dozen stories out of the myriads of manuscripts they'd received and looked at.

Obviously, this tiny number of purchases didn't justify the cost of the time hundreds of editors had spent over the years reading unsolicited submissions. The *Post* then did the obvious thing: The magazine stopped accepting unsolicited manuscripts, and its slush pile became a thing of the past.

The *Post*'s study soon became common knowledge in the world of print publishing, and other magazines as well as many book publishers did similar studies. The results were similarly disappointing from the viewpoint of the author who hoped to become published by finding some route through the slush pile. Many publishing houses stopped accepting unsolicited manuscripts entirely, and others made the reading of the slush pile an extremely low priority.

So where did the houses that ended the practice of maintaining a slush pile find new authors? The same place their analysis said they always had found them: from manuscripts sent them by agents or recommended to them by already-publishing authors or others whose opinions they respected.

Of course, this did nothing to stop or even slow the tide of manuscripts sent out by hopeful writers. It merely shifted it to a different place: the desks of literary agents.

Within a short time every agent listed in the various directories of literary agencies found themselves inundated with thousands of manuscripts, so many that it took a full-time reader or two even to glance at each one, let alone read them all in depth. All of these readers had to be paid, and in the beginning, many agents charged a "reading fee" in order to defray some of the cost of handling their newly swollen slush piles.

Unfortunately, some who weren't legitimate agents at all took a look at the situation and saw a chance to make a great deal of money. By charging a would-be author ten or fifteen dollars to read an unsolicited manuscript and offer "advice" on how to "improve" the manuscript (usually by sending the manuscript back to the writer with two or three boilerplate pages of "one-size-fits-all" critiques), these scamsters quickly gave the entire idea of reading fees a bad name. A professional organization of literary agents, the Association of Authors' Representatives, soon forbade its members from charging reading fees, and many agents then stopped accepting unsolicited manuscripts as well.

The Traditional Role of Agents

This led to the situation we now have, where some agents accept nothing unsolicited, a few still accept anything, but most ask for a one-page summary or pitch letter, from which they winnow a few authors and request either the entire manuscript or a few chapters and an outline.

The end result of all this is that, from the unpublished writer's viewpoint, agents became the "front doors" to the publishing houses and more powerful than ever before. It also faced many writers with the seemingly catch-22 situation that: You can't get an agent without being published, and you can't get published without first getting an agent.

The upshot of all this is that "getting an agent" has become one of the first and most important worries for almost all developing authors. It is generally viewed as the single most critical barrier to overcome in the publishing process.

But we are talking about a new sort of publishing process, aren't we? In the digital revolution, everybody can be a publisher. So how does that change the whole notion of agents?

Do You Need an Agent?

We've got some good news and some bad news. The good news is this: In many, if not most, of the current e-publishing scenarios, you don't need an agent. As for the bad news, if you should happen to find yourself in a situation where you think you need an agent, you probably won't be able to get one. Here's why.

Obviously, if you are your own e-publisher, you don't need an agent. Why would you? You aren't going to negotiate with yourself.

OK, but what about those new, independent e-publishing houses that are springing up all over the Web? Don't they have contracts? And don't you need an agent to negotiate those contracts?

Probably not. In many cases, it won't make much difference anyway, because a lot of e-publishers offer one standard contract on a take-it-or-leave-it basis. When you do find an e-publisher who is willing to negotiate some of its contractual clauses, the changes you are likely to get will be fairly simple.

The Science Fiction and Fantasy Writers of America offer a sample contract for Web publishing that, while not intended to be an actual contract, does cover the points a would-be author should be concerned about, especially in the areas of rights limitations and reversion of rights.

The contract emphasizes that the author grants only the right to publish the specific work on the e-publisher's Web site and that all other rights remain in the hands of the author. It adds a statement about what the e-publisher contracts do: for instance, rendering the work in HTML format. Finally, it states that the author may revoke permission to publish at any time by simply writing or e-mailing a notice of withdrawal to the e-publisher. Read the entire sample contract at www.sfwa.org/contracts/webcontract.htm.

One interesting difference between print publishing and e-publishing is that many e-publishers post a copy of their standard contract right on their Web site. This can be very handy. It allows you to comparison shop among e-publishers, which, in the print world, is the sole province of literary agents, who are well aware of the basic contracts offered by most print publishing houses. The process of comparison is not difficult. If one publisher offers a 10 percent royalty on electronic sales and another offers 40, or one house wants to buy all rights exclusively and forever and another merely wants e-publishing rights with a generous reversion clause (reversion means the ability to get back the rights to your work from the e-publisher in a reasonable time—say, one year), which one would you choose?

We know of no e-publishers that currently offer advances to new authors. All payments made will be royalties paid per sale, not advances against royalties. This removes another area of negotiation that used to be the province of literary agents.

The Traditional Role of Agents

CHAPTER THIRTY-FIVE

IN E-PUBLISHING, AGENTS ARE NO LONGER THE FRONT DOOR

We noted that agents are often viewed as the "front door" to print publishers, and there is some truth to that notion. However, in the world of e-publishing, this is no longer the case. Most e-publishers are wide open to unsolicited submissions from new authors. In fact, most e-publishers plainly state on their Web pages their submissions policy: whether they will look at an entire manuscript, a few chapters and an outline, or whether they require a short "pitch" letter to get the ball rolling. Read these policies carefully, and follow them. There is little more an agent can do for you in this area than you can do for yourself.

To sum up: Just as the digital revolution offers vast new freedom to writers, in particular the ability to self-publish and self-distribute their own work, it has also made many of the traditional functions of the literary agent either not applicable or obsolete.

This may change over time; in fact, it probably will. But as we will now explain, the nature of e-publishing itself will have to undergo some major changes before the necessity of having a traditional agent appears again.

Can You Find an Agent Willing to Represent an E-Book?

Sad to say, you probably won't be able to find a traditional, legitimate literary agent to represent you solely as an e-writer. Here's why.

Agents make their entire incomes from the commission—usually 15 percent—they take of revenues their client-authors receive from contracts they negotiate for them. If an agent negotiates a contract that calls for a $5,000 advance to the author, the agent gets $750 of that. Agents also get 15 percent of all royalties or any other income, such as subsidiary rights sales, that they handle.

Now, $750 may not sound like a great deal, but compared to the possibilities in the current state of e-publishing, it looks pretty good. As we mentioned, we know of no e-publishers that offer cash advances to new authors. We suspect that if there are any such, the advances offered are considerably less than $5,000. Since even most print books don't "earn out" (that means sell enough copies that the author actually earns some royalties over and above the advance), this pretty much eliminates the main source of agent income. Second, and somewhat brutally, most e-books simply don't sell a great number of copies, and while royalties per individual sale may be much higher than those for print books, the number of books currently sold is much lower. Once again, the lack of sales means a loss of potential income for an agent.

Bluntly, there just isn't enough money in the current e-publishing structure to support traditional-style agents, especially in view of the fact that established agents still do a brisk business in the print publishing world. It may seem sad, but it is still true that to such agents, a print bird in the hand is worth much more than two e-published birds in the bush.

Which brings us to the real reason you'll have a tough time finding an agent to represent your e-book solely to e-publishers.

Because of all the reasons we just explained, those few traditional agents who do know something about e-publishing are generally working within the context of subsidiary e-publishing rights negotiated as part of a print book contract with a traditional print publisher. It's true that print houses are expressing a growing interest in the possibilities of e-publishing, and an agent who negotiates with these houses does need to know how to protect and enhance his client's rights in the e-publishing area. But his interest remains directed primarily at print. He won't have much interest, if any, in dealing with pure e-books. In other words, if you are marketing your book to a traditional publisher who also has e-publishing capabilities, you may find an agent to be quite helpful.

The Exception (There's Always One . . .)

It's possible that you may find yourself in a specialized position: You have books previously published in print and are interested in seeing these books reissued as e-books.

This is one situation where an agent can be of great help to you. Print publishers have grown much more knowledgeable about the potential of e-publishing in the last few years, and while they may not yet be ready to leap into e-publishing for themselves, they are at least considering the possibility that they will do so in the future. Because of this, they are looking much harder than previously at trying to retain, or in some cases, manufacture, some rights to e-publish books they've already published in print. This task can become a tricky issue for an author, and in some cases only an agent can sort out the problems.

As an example, a widely publicized court case on this issue involved a lawsuit between Random House (a publisher more Net-savvy than most) and e-publisher Rosetta Books (www.rosettabooks.com) over the notion that Random House owns e-publication rights to every book they've ever contracted to publish. Big-name authors previously published by Random House, whom Rosetta published in e-format, disagreed, so the two publishers went to court. Although Rosetta won the first round, it is obvious that e-publication reprint rights will become a growing and possibly contentious issue in the future.

If you are a previously published author in this situation, you might wish to consult your own agent. If you don't currently have an agent, there is one agency that will go to bat for you; one of the authors of this book, Richard Curtis, a well-known literary agent, (www.curtisagency.com) will attempt to retrieve e-publishing rights from print publishers on a case-by-case basis for authors who wish to reissue their work in digital format.

Scams

As we've mentioned, the Association of Authors' Representatives (www.publishersweekly.com/aar/) does not permit its members to charge fees for reading manuscripts. And as we've demonstrated, the sort of legitimate financial opportunities available to agents in the print world do not exist in e-publishing at this point. Yet a quick search at Google.com returns several thousand hits on literary agents. And some of these agencies do state that they are willing to represent e-books. What gives?

We don't want to tar with too broad a brush, so here are some things to watch out for:
- An agency charges a fee to read an e-book manuscript.
- An agency reads your e-book manuscript and then refers you to a "book doctor," saying that the agent likes your book, but can't do anything with it until the book doctor "cleans it up," or "prepares it for publication."

  A book doctoring service is one that charges you to "fix" or "improve" your manuscript. Such fees can often be hundreds, even thousands, of dollars.
- The agency offers, for a fee, to do the book doctoring job.

Any or all of these situations should raise a red flag with an e-book author. Legitimate agents make their money by selling the work of their clients, not selling supposed "services" to their clients.

Where to Find More Information About Agents

Here are some places on the Web you can go to learn more about finding and working with literary agents.

- **The Association of Authors' Representatives:** (www.publishers weekly.com/aar/). The AAR maintains a list of their member agents here. Members must subscribe to a strict code of ethics, which is also listed here. There is also other information and helpful links for authors.

- **Preditors and Editors:** (www.sfwa.org/preditors/pubagent .htm) maintains an extensive list of agencies, along with recommendations and a wealth of information about agents.

  For some odd reason, while the agents are listed alphabetically, they are alphabetized by the first name of the agent or agency: for instance, Richard Curtis Associates, Inc. is listed under "R" for "Richard," not "C" for "Curtis."

- **AuthorLink:** (www.authorlink.com/agents.html). AuthorLink maintains listings for hundreds of agents and agencies. While offering no judgments or recommendations on individual agents or agencies, each listing does provide a wealth of valuable information.

  The AuthorLink Web site itself is a valuable resource for e-book authors and publishers. Check it out at www.authorlink .com. Registration is required to access much of this site.

Aside from a few specific exceptions, you don't need an agent in order to e-publish your e-book. And that's another benefit to e-publishing. No more agent worries. That should be worth the price of admission alone.

CHAPTER THIRTY-SIX

THE TWO SIDES OF DIGITAL RIGHTS MANAGEMENT

We've already touched on the general issue of digital rights management, also known by the acronym DRM. We'll go into the subject a bit more deeply now because DRM will affect all e-publishers in the future, at least to some extent, whether they make use of it or not.

First, the definition of the term, to refresh your memory: DRM is technology that allows an e-publisher to determine how the content of his book may be used. That's the simple summary. In more detail, DRM technology can allow e-publishers to decide how or whether readers can *obtain* their content, make *copies* of it, *redistribute* it, use it on *different platforms* and to exert control in other areas of content delivery as well. DRM technology attempts to provide tools that will let you determine how your e-books are obtained, read and otherwise made use of.

The state of e-publishing today is already complicated and difficult enough for the average reader, even without DRM considerations. "What file format should I get? Do I buy a stand-alone book reader? Or maybe one of those software versions? Will it run on my computer? Why are e-books so darned expensive from one e-publisher and so cheap from another? How do I find the blasted things in the first place?"

Add to these perfectly legitimate complaints the further complication that the e-book some reader did manage to find, buy and try to read will not, for some reason, allow him to print out a few pages. Or transfer the e-book to a different computer. Or loan or give the file to a friend. Nevertheless, in order to control how your book's content is being used, it is important to understand the complicated concept of DRM and the DRM technologies that help protect your book.

In his excellent article, "Digital Rights Management's Hidden Dangers" (www.zdnet.com/zdnn/stories/comment/0,5859,26844 35,00.html), Andreas Pfeiffer clearly explains the two bedrocks upon which DRM now stands. The first is the rights of the content publisher. The second is the rights of the content consumer. Pfeiffer and others have pointed out the basic conflict between these two. In a nutshell, the more tightly the e-publisher tries to control the use of his content, the more inconvenient it can become for the consumer to make use of that content. And this is the basic dichotomy you, as an e-publisher or e-writer, will have to contend with, both now and in the future.

Here's the problem: Major print publishing houses are extremely interested in making use of the opportunities presented by the digital revolution to lower the costs and increase the distribution of their inventories. And why wouldn't they be? They can see the same advantages for themselves that we can see for the individual e-publisher. But print publishers, and also pure e-publishers, have costs, and those costs must be covered with something left over—called "profit"—in order for these publishers to remain in business. And one of the biggest threats to the notion of profits in any kind of publishing is that of unlimited free copying of the publishers' wares. In other words, is there some way they can minimize the risk to their bottom line involved in presenting e-books in digital format to the general public? And if *you* are hoping to sell your e-books online, this is a question you must also consider.

The perceived necessity on the part of print and e-publishers to be able to control the distribution of their content (which constitutes what they have to sell, their *intellectual property*) gained even more urgency with the recent example of Napster, where millions of copies of copyright-protected music were traded freely across the Internet. Print publishers are wary (or terrified) of finding themselves in a similar situation. Many e-publishers also worry about having control over their e-books.

The concerns of the publishers ultimately led them to concentrate on content control from a distribution point of view.

However, as we note, there is another side to consider: that of the consumer who is at the other end of the publishing chain. To make the problem a bit clearer, let's consider what happens when you buy a print book.

You take the book to the store's checkout counter, pay for it and walk away. The book is now *yours*, at least that one physical thing we call a book. You can read that book. If you desire, you can scribble notes in the margins. You could run it through a photocopier (as long as the copy is for your own use). You could resell your copy to somebody else, or you could lend it or give it to a friend. You take all of these abilities for granted, since they are part of the publishing model that has existed for centuries. From your point of view, the book you bought is yours, and you can do pretty much whatever you'd like with it.

But do you really have the right to do anything with "your" book? In order to properly answer the question, we first have to distinguish between the physical manifestation, the paper book you bought, and the story printed on those paper pages. Is the book the object, or the content? Put it a different way: Would you buy a book that consisted of nothing but blank pages?

Obviously, you wouldn't. So the "book" isn't really the object itself. It's the content, the intellectual property that somebody— that's you!—sweated and dreamed and worked on to create. In

The Two Sides of Digital Rights Management

the end, that paper thing with all the pages you hold in your hand is nothing more than a delivery system for the content, no different in concept than a digital file that displays on your computer. What matters is the stuff you read via that delivery system. And can you do anything you'd like with that, simply because you've bought one chunk of dead trees with a copy of the content printed on it?

Of course you can't. Not legally, at least, and as a practical matter, not very easily, either. For instance: Could you make a copy of your book, take it to a printer, have ten thousand new copies printed and bound, and sell them yourself? Only if you'd like a quick visit from some very nasty antipiracy lawyers. Not to mention that it would take a lot of work and cost you a lot of money in the first place to do something like that.

How about if you write your own book based on the book you bought, but you change all the names, do some paraphrasing here and there, plaster your name at the top as the author and publish that?

Nope. That's called plagiarism, and it will bring you a different pack of legal pitbulls snapping at your heels (or some other body part—maybe your wallet).

So it should be obvious that you can't do anything you'd like with "your" book. And this is the conundrum faced by publishers and creators—the digital revolution makes it incredibly easy to do these sorts of things.

Yet book buyers are used to being able to do pretty much what they wish with their physical books—and that is the mindset they bring to the purchase of e-books, as well.

"I bought it, it's mine," many e-book buyers say. "Why can't I give my copy to my friend? Or lend it to her? Why can't I make notes on the edges or print a copy out on paper? Why can't I make another copy of the file and e-mail it to a friend or cut and paste a section I like and do likewise?"

All of these functions and abilities can be controlled by DRM technology. But do publishers really want to use such stringent controls?

As Andreas Pfeiffer puts it in the article cited on page 178, "What's wrong with DRM? Quite simple: It is mainly concerned with the illegal use of material and cares little about the lawful customer."

Yes, you may have good reasons for wanting to protect your e-books in some way. But in the end, both print and e-publishing are about distributing books into the hands of customers; and when a business deals with customers, in almost every significant instance, the customer is always right. Pfeiffer goes on to say, "The first concern of any DRM solution should be to make sure that the intended user of the content doesn't experience any constraint on his legitimate use of the content he has acquired. Any system that doesn't offer the customer this basic consideration is doomed."

The struggle between the two sides of DRM and how it turns out will very likely have a great deal to do with how successful e-publishing, even free e-publishing, becomes in the future.

Why? Well, for one thing, without a viable business model for publishers who already control much of the attractive content, as well as for those who will create it in the future who do hope to be able to sell it over the Internet, not much of such content will be rendered into digital formats. In other words, without supply to drive demand, the entire field won't advance much. And we need those advances, in hardware and software technology, in distribution and marketing techniques, in order for the entire field of e-publishing not only to grow, but to remain viable at all.

Finding the Best Compromise

So what's an e-publisher to do? Both sides of the e-publishing equation have legitimate concerns, and those concerns are obviously not entirely compatible. Nevertheless, we'll take our chances and venture some advice: We feel that the best course for e-publishers to take is to make the most limited use of DRM possible that remains consistent with equally limited protection concerns. In other words, allow your reader to do as many of the things they are used to doing with "their" print books as you can. We would suggest that you always allow your e-books to be printed, to be loaned or given away and to be annotated (those scribbles in the margin that so many like to do).

As we've noted before, DRM technology, like almost everything else in the world of e-publishing, is a constantly moving target. The technologies of today will differ from the technologies of tomorrow. In the meantime, if you must err, err on the side of openness. Don't try to force your readers to change how they think of books or what they can do with them, because you won't succeed. All you'll manage to do is drive them back into the print world they already know and understand . . . and love.

CHAPTER THIRTY-SEVEN

ISSUES SURROUNDING INTELLECTUAL PROPERTY

In the preceding chapter, we discussed the concept of protecting and/or restricting the use of intellectual property. One of the unexpected side effects of the digital revolution has been the pressure it has put on the traditional model of intellectual property protection, particularly in terms of the ease of duplication and distribution made possible by the Internet and the difficulty of enforcing copyright law. What has occurred is an effect known as the Law of Unintended Consequences, which can loosely be expressed as, "When we did *this*, we sure didn't expect *that* to happen."

What Is Property?

The average person is accustomed to thinking of property as something tangible, something physical that he owns—land, automobiles, houses, jewelry, even . . . books. For most people, the concept of something intangible, that has no physical existence yet is still property, becomes hard to grasp.

And small wonder this is so. The notion "I make widgets and sell them for a living" is simple, natural and highly intuitive. It is how the vast majority of people understand the world of business: They make things.

In fact, until quite recently in human history, this was the only understanding of property. The concept of intellectual property is quite a latecomer to the world of human ideas, although by the time the Founding Fathers met to write the United States Constitution, it was well established.

Article I of the Constitution states that one of the duties of the U.S. Government shall be: "To promote the progress of science and useful arts, by securing for limited times to authors and inventors the exclusive right to their respective writings and discoveries."

Congress carried out this mandate by establishing various copyright, trademark and patent laws designed to protect the rights of creators of intellectual property "to their respective writings and discoveries."

Definition of Intellectual Property
The 'Lectric Law Library (www.lectlaw.com/def/
i051.htm) defines intellectual property thusly:

"Property that can be protected under federal law, including copyrightable works, discoveries, and inventions. Such property would include novels, sound recordings, a new type of mousetrap, or a cure for a disease."

While this definition may be subject to further legal refinement in specific cases, it will do well enough for the purposes of our discussion. For a complete and extensive explication of U.S. copyright law, the U.S. Copyright Office maintains a Web site at www.loc.gov/copyright/. It is well worth a visit.

Why Is Intellectual Property So Important?

For much of human history, a person's intellectual property wasn't seen as important—at least not in the sense that such property was formally protected by law. The notion that a singer like Homer, chanting his tales of the fall of Troy around a campfire, somehow "owned" the words he sang would have been considered ridiculous. In fact, it wouldn't have been considered at all. And during the Middle Ages, the legions of monks who labored over hundreds of manuscripts, making copy after copy for monastic libraries, would have been similarly puzzled by the idea.

However, even then, folks engaged in more mundane activities understood the need to protect the expression of ideas. The most common form of such understanding involved trade secrets. If the Potter's Guild in the city of Verona discovered a new way to make thin-walled porcelain, they kept the method secret as long as they could because it gave them a trade advantage. They knew how to make something nobody else could duplicate. But what they protected was not the porcelains themselves, it was the idea, the knowledge, of how to make them. This knowledge was more valuable than the tangible products themselves, though you couldn't see the knowledge or taste it or hold it in your hand.

As humanity advanced, such intellectual property became more and more important to the progress of human living, and eventually this came to be recognized by governments and protected by them. Finally, protections originally designed to guard trade secrets were extended to creative works like books and stories and to such odd innovations as software.

Today, in the age of the information economy, ideas and knowledge have become even more important. If, for instance, software were not a protected class, much of the Information Age simply would not have occurred. Developing software takes a huge amount of time and money; without copyright protection affording companies a chance to earn a profit on their outlays, the outlays wouldn't be made in the first place. And writers today wouldn't be able to use word processors, because they wouldn't exist. Thus, this once-disregarded form of property has become the wheel that turns almost every aspect of our daily lives, and the ability to buy and sell such property is critical, not just to our current existence, but to progress itself.

Art and Commerce

As an e-book writer, you create intellectual property. As an e-book publisher, you package, distribute and market it. And as a creator, packager, distributor and marketer of intellectual property, your property is generally protected by most modern governments in the form of *copyright laws.*

But what do such laws protect, and what is copyrightable intellectual property protected from?

In terms of U.S. copyright law, an author cannot protect an idea but can protect the unique expression of that idea. For instance, an author might have an idea for a book that involves submarine warfare. You can't copyright that idea. But if you write *Red Storm Rising*, as Tom Clancy did, you can then copyright that unique expression of the idea of submarine warfare, just as another author, writing a different novel involving submarine warfare, can also copyright his masterpiece.

What Does Copyright Regulate?

As we've touched on previously, the heart of copyright is the *right to make copies.* In essence, you control the right to allow others to make copies of your intellectual property, which are the books, stories, songs, poems and essays you write.

With the advent of the digital age, the ability to make unlimited copies of computer files has naturally placed great pressure on the protections afforded intellectual property by copyright laws. By this we mean that while the legal protections still exist, the ease by which they can be violated does seem to present a threat to their effectiveness.

> **DID YOU KNOW?**
>
> What you write is protected under U.S. copyright law the moment you put words on paper or on a computer hard disk? When you create intellectual property, it is protected from the moment of creation.

The Three Es

Bill Hill, the man in charge of Microsoft's development of Clear-Type, the screen-enhancing component of Microsoft Reader, often speaks of what he calls the "Three Es"— enforcement, engineering and education—as a combined method of strengthening intellectual property protections.

Microsoft has experience in this area; their entire business is based on the creation and sale of intellectual property in the form of software. Some observers have estimated that as much as 40 percent of all Microsoft software in use today is pirated—illegal copies. Hill's approach to e-book infringement is based on Microsoft's current approach to infringement on their software.

Enforcement

In Hill's view, this doesn't necessarily mean using legal tactics to go after the individual infringer—the reader who, either intentionally or inadvertently, acquires an illicit copy of an e-book. It does, however, include making use of legal means of enforcement to combat large-scale piracy of intellectual property. This approach is somewhat similar to that used now with videotapes. Despite the blood-curdling warnings on each tape, a SWAT team isn't going to kick in your door if you make a copy of a tape here and there, even if the copyright is violated in so doing. However, if you are discovered making hundreds of copies for resale, you can expect a visit from men and women wearing badges.

If you are a small e-publisher or a self-e-publisher, this may not matter to you, simply because you don't have the resources to pursue legal penalties against those who infringe on your works. However, larger e-publishers will be able to do so; if you have licensed your work to such a publisher, you may benefit from the financial and legal "clout" they can bring to bear against the theft of intellectual property in the same way you benefit from similar strength in the print publishing world.

Engineering

This step concerns the technical protections built into e-book hardware and software, including digital rights management. While it is true that no system is entirely crackproof, designers do try to make it difficult for the average reader to violate copyright protection. Yes, a dedicated, knowledgeable hacker, given enough time and effort, can probably crack any protection scheme out there. But since these folks make up only the tiniest percentage of the overall readership, designers more or less write them off and aim their intellectual property safeguards at the vast bulk of the market.

As an e-publisher, you should be aware that certain formats offer greater technical protections against infringement than do others. For instance, Microsoft Reader format can be made much more secure than a simple text file.

Education

We like this one. Why? Because it relies on the notion of the essential goodness and honesty of human nature. The theory here is that a lot of small-scale intellectual property infringement is done by folks who simply don't know that what they're doing is a form of theft that, even if it weren't illegal, would still be wrong. The hope is that by educating folks to the importance of protecting intellectual property and explaining why it is harmful to all of us to misappropriate an intellectual property creator's property rights, most people's natural tendency toward honesty and fair play will lead them to respect copyright protections.

How You Can Help Protect Yourself and Others

Unless you're already a software or hardware designer, you can't really do much with the engineering end of the equation. And your participation in the enforcement component will probably be fairly limited as well. However, you can do a great deal to advance the education element. Here's how.

- Make sure you always put a notice of copyright on your material. This is easily done. All it takes is something like: Copyright SomeAuthor (your name) 2001 (or whatever the year of creation is). This serves notice to the reader that the work is protected by copyright law. Most will have only the fuzziest notion what that means, but for some, it will be all the notice required.

- Beneath your copyright notice, if you are self-publishing, add a short summary of the rights you are granting to the reader, in plain English. For instance: "You may copy this material for your own use, lend a single copy at one time and print out a single copy." Or, "You may reprint this material for a fee to be negotiated between you and the author."

- If you really want to go the extra mile, you might consider adding a brief bit of educational material concerning copyright, as in: "This e-book is intellectual property protected by copyright. This means it may be a violation of civil or criminal law to make copies for other than personal use without the permission of the author. Authors of intellectual property depend on copyright to protect their work and allow them to earn income by selling it. Without such protection, there would be much less incentive to create such works in the first place. By respecting the author's rights, you can help to create a better environment for all creative endeavors."

Does all this sound a bit naïve to you? Well, perhaps. But we believe that most people want to do the right thing and will do so as long as they know what the right thing is.

Maybe that makes us Pollyannas. But we like that better than the alternative.

PART FIVE

Marketing and Distributing Your E-Book

CHAPTER THIRTY-EIGHT

AVENUES FOR DISTRIBUTING YOUR E-BOOK

P eople who aren't well versed in what is often rightly called the "dismal science" of economics sometimes confuse the notions of distribution and marketing. It's easy enough to do. Marketing does, in fact, occasionally overlap into the world of distribution, and vice versa.

However, in the case of e-publishing, in order to gain a workable understanding of both, we need for practical purposes to separate them.

Distribution: The Plumbing Beneath the Market

When you *market* your e-book, you draw people's attention to it in such a way as to encourage them to obtain it. *Distribution* deals with how and where they obtain your book once marketing makes them aware of it and convinces them they want it.

You don't go to a department store to buy a car, nor do you go to the local Ford dealership to pick up a crate of apples. Department stores are distribution channels for a variety of personal and household items, just as auto dealerships distribute cars and grocery stores distribute food. Every item has a recognizable distribution outlet—and the outlet for e-books is the e-bookstores.

There are thousands of e-bookstores on the Web, some selling only a handful of books, but the two largest and best known are Amazon.com (www.amazon.com) and Barnes & Noble (www.bn.com). In addition, superstore Borders sells books through Amazon.com (www.borders.com). The primary business of all of these huge bookstores (Amazon.com at one time billed itself as "the world's biggest bookstore") is the sale and delivery of print books. However, all of them also handle e-books; and if you go about it properly—and we tell you how to do this—they will stock your e-book as well.

How to Get Your Book Stocked in E-Bookstores

In order to get your book distributed in the various e-bookstores, it's important to know the traditional steps publishers take in order for a bookstore to carry their products.

International Standard Book Numbers (ISBN)

The frequently asked questions (FAQ) page at the ISBN.org Web site (www.isbn.org/standards/home/isbn/us/isbnqa.html#Q10) defines an ISBN as:

"The International Standard Book Number (ISBN) is a 10-digit number that uniquely identifies books and book-like products published internationally."

As to the purpose of an ISBN, ISBN.org says:

"The purpose of the ISBN is to establish and identify one title or edition of a title from one specific publisher and is unique to that edition, allowing for more efficient marketing of products by booksellers, libraries, universities, wholesalers and distributors."

Do You Need an ISBN for Your E-Book?

It depends. If you have self-published your e-book and are marketing it only from your own Web page, probably not. But to go much beyond this, you should realize that there is a large, well-developed and long-standing system for classifying books that is used by all bookstores, libraries and other distributors, and the system is based on ISBN identification. If you want to make use of the marketing and distribution muscle of e-bookstores like Amazon.com and Barnes & Noble, you will need to obtain ISBNs for each of your e-books.

Another reason for obtaining an ISBN is that this number allows bookstores and libraries to use a single reference to find lots of information about your book, including the price, a short description of its content, and how and where to order it.

How Can You Obtain an ISBN?

If your e-books are published by an e-publisher, they should take care of such details as obtaining ISBNs for you. Otherwise you'll need to obtain one yourself.

Keep in mind that ISBNs are issued for every format you publish your book in: for instance, the e-book would get one number; a print-on-demand paper book version would get another; and if you have arranged to have your book printed locally in hardcover, that edition would require a third.

If your home or office is in the United States and your e-book is being published here, you must go to the U.S. ISBN agency responsible for issuing ISBN publisher prefixes. That agency is R.R. Bowker. They maintain a Web site at www.bowker.com. If you aren't a U.S. resident, you can also find links to international ISBN agencies on that site.

ISBNs are issued in minimum blocks of ten. All the forms necessary for application can be found at the Web site. You can either fill them out online (we recommend this method—it's faster) or you can download a printed form, fill it out and mail it in.

The minimum fee for ten ISBNs is $225 for regular processing fees. If you wish to expedite the process, you must pay an additional

$50. Is the extra charge worth it? The ISBN Web site does not specify how long the standard processing procedure takes, but it does guarantee that the expedited version will give you a turn-around "within 72 business hours of receipt of your ISBN Publisher Prefix and ISBN log book (provided there are no problems with the application)."

If you are in a hurry, spend the extra fifty bucks.

What Do You Do Once You Have an ISBN?

Once you receive your block of ISBNs, return to the R.R. Bowker Web site to assign one of the numbers to each of your editions and enter publishing and purchasing details. Bowker maintains a separate Web site for this process at www.bowkerlink.com/correcti ons/common/home.asp.

Entering this information ensures that your books will be listed in Bowker's various databases, as well as in their famous *Books in Print*.

Make sure you do this. If you don't, your books won't automatically be listed in *Books in Print*, and you certainly won't be getting your money's worth, given that every bookstore and library uses *Books in Print* to find ordering and content information on books. Without that listing, your book may as well not exist, at least as far as these distribution channels go.

If you order the minimum number of ISBNs, you will receive ten. You can use them one at a time or all at once. However, once you've assigned all of them, you have to purchase more, at the same terms, if you need them. The next level that Bowker offers is one hundred ISBNs for $800, which is much cheaper *per number*, but still considerably more expensive up front.

Worse, strictly interpreted as *one number per edition format*, your needs can mount quickly. For instance, if you publish your e-book in Adobe eBook Reader format, Microsoft Reader format, Night Kitchen format and plain text, Bowker regards each of these as a separate edition requiring a separate ISBN. Add POD format and, perhaps, CD-ROM and hardcover, and you need seven ISBNs for this one book. If you have two or three books you want to e-publish, you can see how this could mount up quickly.

The ISBN system is a long-established method of classifying books that dates from centuries of print tradition. As such, it is becoming something of a relic in the digital age, especially with its insistence on requiring a separate number for each format.

Given that, unlike print books, e-book formats change and grow more quickly than Topsy, there is already a great deal of unrest regarding ISBNs among e-publishers. Eventually, the ISBN system will change in response or possibly disappear entirely, replaced by something more flexible and responsive to the needs of the digital age.

Until that time, though, it is still the way books are classified, and if you want to make use of both traditional and digital distribution methods and outlets, you will need ISBNs.

Once you've obtained your ISBN, you are ready to approach the online e-book sellers. We'll start with Amazon.com.

Sell Your E-Books at Amazon.com

Amazon is truly the Big Kahuna of online bookselling. More people who buy books online keep a handy link to this bookstore than any other. So it makes sense that if you want your e-books available in the most obvious places, Amazon.com is where you want to start.

And where you want to start at Amazon.com is at their Amazon Advantage program for booksellers, which is located at www.amazon.com/exec/obidos/subst/partners/direct/book-benefits.html/104-7104368-2538348. On this page or linked to it is everything you need to know about selling your e-books on Amazon.com.

Here are some highlights about the Amazon Advantage program for Books, quoted from the Web site we just mentioned:

- To enroll in Amazon.com Advantage, you must have an e-mail account and Web access, you must be located in North America, and you must have worldwide distribution rights to the title you want to enroll. In addition:
- If your title is a book, it must have an ISBN that is printed on the book.
- Each title, whether book, CD, video or DVD, must also satisfy Amazon.com's suitability standards. These standards currently relate to quality, value, subject matter, production standards and compliance with intellectual property laws. In no event will any title that Amazon deems, at its sole discretion, to be pornographic be accepted into the program.

Amazon has special *marketing forms* you can fill in that will help you make your e-book stand out from others. You can also include a picture of the book cover, an interview with the author (that would be you) and other tools to increase your sales.

The Amazon Advantage program costs nothing to join, but there are fees, and they seem to be fairly steep.

Here's the skinny from Amazon:

- Amazon.com will automatically issue you a check for copies sold during a given month at the end of the following month. For instance, if a copy sells any time during the month of January, Amazon.com will issue and mail you a check by the last day of February. This allows Amazon to account for any returns [it] may have on your title.
- All payments will be made in U.S. dollars.
- For books, Amazon will pay you 45 percent of the publisher's list price or of the suggested retail price you selected. This is equivalent to a 55 percent purchase discount.
- For a $8.99 book, Amazon pays you $4.05
- For a $10.99 book, Amazon pays you $4.95
- For a $12.99 book, Amazon pays you $5.85

- For a $14.99 book, Amazon pays you $6.75
- For a $16.99 book, Amazon pays you $7.65
- For a $20.99 book, Amazon pays you $9.45

If this seems a bit dear to you, keep this in mind: 45 percent of something is a heck of a lot more than 100 percent of nothing. To sharpen the perspective even further, consider this: If, instead of publishing your e-book yourself and distributing it through Amazon.com, you license publication to an e-publisher, you will receive a *royalty* that will very likely be, at best, 40 percent of the cover price—5 percent *less* than your net from Amazon.

Amazon also simplifies the e-publisher's accounting chores by providing extensive sales and accounting information on a monthly basis.

Amazon.com is the single biggest engine of book sales on the World Wide Web. Further, the site is extremely well designed and customer friendly, with excellent search facilities that make your books easy to find.

If you are self-publishing your e-books, we highly recommend that you look into Amazon's Advantage program for books.

Sell Your E-Books at Barnes & Noble

All of the advantages that apply to distributing your e-books through Amazon also apply to Barnes & Noble's online operation.

Since that is the case, you probably wonder whether bn.com has a program for authors similar to Amazon.com's Advantage program.

They do. Start at www.barnesandnoble.com/help/pub_wewant_tosell.asp?userid=0ED0Y3CXAB.

Since page locations seem to change even more often than e-book formats, you may find that this link doesn't work. If so, simply go to bn.com's *help* page at www.barnesandnoble.com/help/

help.asp, and click on the links under the section heading, *For Publishers and Authors.*

Barnes & Noble also offers their own print-on-demand service to authors and publishers and maintains a special section for e-books. Also, like Amazon.com, Barnes & Noble's Web site provides sales and accounting data regularly, which is one less task you have to worry about.

Each section of the publishers and authors help pages offers e-mail links you can use to get further information, if anything seems unclear to you.

Sell Your E-Books at Borders

Borders is a true testament to the ever changing nature of the Web. While they once had their own Web site and their own method of working with e-publishers and authors of e-books, they are now partnered with Amazon.com. Their site can be reached by typing in www.borders.com or through www.amazon.com.

Taking advantage of the ability to add your books to these major bookselling Web sites may seem like a lot of work, but if you do take the time and effort, you'll be rewarded with the knowledge that you are listed in the three outlets that sell about 90 percent of all books sold over the Internet.

This isn't small potatoes. Listing your books at www.amazon.com, www.barnesandnoble.com and www.borders.com vastly increases your chances of success. So take a deep breath, hitch up your pants and "just *do* it."

You won't be disappointed.

CHAPTER THIRTY-NINE

SELF-DISTRIBUTION METHODS

emember, distribution involves various ways of moving your e-book from here to there, "here" being wherever a copy of the e-book is maintained and "there" being into your reader's possession.

Listing your e-book on one of the major online bookstores is one such method. There are many others.

Self-Distribution

This method of distribution is easy. Potential readers come to you and ask you to "send" your e-book to them. This may take the form of a financial transaction, or it may be simply a case of "ask and you shall receive—free."

In any case, once the initial part of the transaction has been completed, it's then your job, as an e-publisher, to put the goods into your readers' hands. Here are four ways to self-distribute your e-books.

Web Site Access

You may set up a distribution channel directly from your Web site, your own private bookstore on the Web, where folks can download a copy of your e-book to their own computer. We've already discussed several ways to do this in section three.

E-Mail

In some cases, you may wish to simply e-mail a copy of the e-book to your reader. This is done by attaching the file to an e-mail, generally in ZIPped form. A "ZIPped file" is simply one that has been compressed to a much smaller file, using a small software program to do the job. The reason you want to do this is that smaller files make it easier and faster for your reader to receive the e-mail containing the file. There are many programs available that let you compress your e-book files into ZIP files. The one we prefer is called WinZip, available at www.winzip.com. WinZip costs twenty-nine dollars, but you can download a free evaluation version to try before you buy.

The e-mail to which you attach your file should contain a subject line something like: "Your E-Book Delivery:Title." The body of the e-mail should tell your customers whatever they need to know in order to read the book. If it needs to be unZIPped, tell them how. Or if the file is in some special format the readers need additional software to access, tell them what it is and where to get a copy for themselves.

Examples: .lit files require the free Microsoft Reader. .pdf files need one of the forms of Adobe file readers, either Acrobat Reader or Adobe eBook Reader.

Give customers an e-mail address they can write to if they have problems. Use an antivirus program to check your e-book file before you send it out, and tell your readers that the attached file has been scanned and is virus free. It can be a mean world out there on the Internet, and one can never be too careful.

And one last thing: Be sure, somewhere in your e-mail, to thank your readers for taking the time and effort to read your e-book.

After all, that's only fair, don't you think? And who knows? They may come back to read your next e-book. You are working on that one right now, aren't you?

CD-ROM

Some folks are only about halfway into the digital mindset. They're willing to take the step beyond print and read an electronic file instead of a handful of paper, but they still want something tangible they can hold in their hand or store away. Some readers just feel better knowing that, while they don't own a real book, they do have something that exists in the real world.

Copying your e-book onto a CD-ROM and sending the CD scratches that itch. Most modern computers come already equipped with drives that can read CD-ROMs, and the media itself is light, strong and durable. And CD-ROMs should outlast most common paper books.

We won't go into the technical aspects of what you need in order to copy a file onto a CD-ROM—in the parlance, this is known as "burning" a CD—but the necessary equipment and software to accomplish this is ubiquitous. You need a "CD Read-Write" drive, usually called a CD-RW drive. Many models are available from as many different manufacturers, and the price keeps coming down every day. You can now find everything from inexpensive models for under a hundred dollars to top-of-the-line equipment at three hundred or more. If all you want to do is copy e-book files onto CD-ROMs, you don't need the high-priced spread. As an added bonus, almost all CD-RW drives include basic software to let you do your copying. Finally, the blank CDs onto which you do your copying are not at all expensive. Expect to pay less than a dollar per CD in packs of ten or more. You can package your CD in either a paper slip-case or spend a bit more and use plastic "jewel boxes." And for a final fillip, you might consider creating an attractive "cover jacket" for your book, if you do decide to use the plastic cases.

Floppy Disks

"Floppies" are the way files were transferred from one computer to another for many years, and there is certainly no problem in using them for the same purpose today. Current basic floppy disks hold 1.3 megabytes of data, usually far more than you will need for a single e-book. Of course, if your e-book is really big, you can always break it up into separate files and copy it onto more than one disk. Floppies are light, durable, easy and inexpensive to pack and ship, and quite cheap. Buy them in bulk for pennies per disk. Best of all, you don't need extra equipment or software to make "floppy copies" of your e-book.

ABOUT COVER ART

No matter which way you decide to distribute your book, you'll want the entire package to be attractive. One crucial aspect of the package is the cover. Whether it's a cover on the case of a CD-ROM or a JPG on your Web site, you'll want it to look as professional as possible. You can create your own cover art using one of the many paint or draw programs available. Windows operating systems include a very basic program called "Paint," but this application is quite limited. Here are some other possibilities you might consider.

- Adobe makes many high-end image editing programs, including the well-known *Adobe Photoshop*. At six hundred dollars, however, *Photoshop* is expensive, in part because it offers many high-end features of more interest to a professional image designer. However, if you want one of the most powerful of this type of program, see www.adobe.com/products/photoshop/. There are versions of *Photoshop* for both Windows and Mac operating systems.

- Jasc Software's *Paint Shop Pro* offers a wealth of features that will let you do just about anything you can think of in terms of art and design and costs around a hundred dollars. Paint Shop Pro is available at www.jasc.com. *Paint Shop Pro* only runs on Windows operating systems.

- If you use an Apple computer, you may find that the well-known *Apple-Works* software suite, which includes solid drawing and painting programs, will give you all the image design capabilities you need. *Apple-Works* costs less than eighty dollars and is available from Apple at www.apple.com/appleworks/.

Using Ready-Made Images for Your Cover

There are hundreds of collections of images on the Internet. Since new ones appear almost daily and old ones often change or shift addresses, the best way to find such archives is to put the phrase "image archives" into a good search engine and then check several of the results.

The U.S. government maintains many archives of pictures from its various endeavors including the space program, wildlife management, national parks and dozens of other subjects. Many of these pictures are not subject to copyright restrictions, which means you are free to use them as you will.

Private archives sometimes offer art that is free to the user. More often, there will be some charge for licensing the use of a piece of artwork. Generally, these fees are quite small.

Another possibility is that you might see something you like used as an illustration or decorative art on a Web page somewhere. There are no guarantees, but there is nothing wrong in e-mailing the owner or Web master of that page to inquire if the art is available for licensing. Explain that you plan to use it as the cover of your book. You may be pleasantly surprised when the artist grants you the free use of the work or requests only a small fee for use.

CHAPTER FORTY

ALTERNATE METHODS OF DISTRIBUTION

Libraries

Libraries are a distribution channel that most e-publishers don't give much consideration to—and that will soon be a mistake.

Libraries are huge purchasers of books, though we have to admit their e-book acquisition and distribution models are not yet fully developed. Nonetheless, some possibilities do exist to get your work into library digital book programs.

The reading model for libraries is somewhat different than that for the general public. From a publisher's point of view, the idea is to sell one book to one reader. But from a librarian's point of view, they buy one book for many readers, although the reading is done by consecutive readers. Because of this, libraries often pay more per book than a regular purchaser, and some of the developing models for e-book purchases by libraries take cognizance of this— especially since an e-book could potentially be read by an infinite number of readers at the same time.

There is no centralized distribution channel that provides e-books to libraries as Amazon.com or BarnesandNobel.com do to individual readers. However, that doesn't mean there may not be one coming soon. In the meantime, there are two companies, which are discussed below, you should keep an eye on. Neither of them yet, to our knowledge, is open to individual e-book self-publishers, but both do make alliances with established publishers of one sort or another, and they may well open up to a wider range of e-books in the future.

E-BOOKS IN LIBRARIES

Roberto Esteves, the man in charge of new and electronic media for the San Francisco Public Library, tells us that he makes use of two companies that have been designed to cater to libraries in the digital age.

www.netlibrary.com

netLibrary's "Overview for Publishers" (www.netlibrary.com/publisher_index.asp) provides this information:

Publishing is your core business and you know it well. Creating and distributing electronic versions of your books to libraries is our core business, and the proof of how well we know that business is substantial:

- More than 30,000 complete titles are currently available in e-book form, representing a broad range of subject areas that meets the needs of thousands of diverse library customers, including academic, public, corporate, K–12, and special libraries.
- Alliances with major publishers who enjoy monthly revenues for the e-books sold through netLibrary—millions paid to publishers to date.
- Publishing, content, librarian and cataloging teams of experienced industry professionals dedicated to building, developing, and promoting the collections and titles provided by our publishers.
- A business model that ensures the integrity of your brand, your content format, and your revenue base.
- A collaborative process that recognizes it's no longer about the Internet as a vehicle for accessing data in "quantity" . . . it's really more about

organizing and effectively distributing the kind of quality and value—leveraging Internet technology—that we both know will sell best.

- A comprehensive marketing program designed to promote e-books all year long with flexibility for featuring specific publishers and specific titles within certain marketing venues.

netLibrary does not yet appear to be open to individually self-published e-books, but that may well change in the future. We suggest you keep checking in periodically to find out if it does.

www.ebrary.com

The second source Mr. Esteves mentioned is a place called ebrary, at www.ebrary.com.

ebrary defines its role vis à vis libraries thusly:

"ebrary's technology augments the library's services and provides its patrons with access to the complete text contained within published, authoritative content. ebrary provides a powerful search engine that utilizes traditional bibliographic information. Unquestionably, the computer is far superior at finding and interacting with information than the printed page. However, the printed page still reigns as far as readability and portability are concerned. ebrary seeks to augment the information held within printed documents, as opposed to replacing it."

As with netLibrary, ebrary.com doesn't yet appear to be open to self-e-publishers, but as fast as the e-publishing scene is changing, it won't hurt for you to keep an eye on them. In the future, either or both ebrary.com or netLibrary may become a powerful distribution channel carrying your e-books onto the electronic "shelves" of thousands of libraries.

Independent Bookstores

There are thousands of independent bookstores in the "brick-and-mortar" world. As a group, indy booksellers account for one out of every seven books sold. While times have been tough for them of late in their competition with the large chain outlets, they are beginning to participate in the e-book revolution.

Some independent booksellers maintain their own Web sites through which they sell print books and, in some cases, e-books. Their operation may be strictly a local affair, with all stocking decisions made by the bookstore itself. Generally, such operations are fielded by the larger independents. The best way to find out if any of your local independent booksellers are interested in stocking your e-book is to call them and ask.

If you'd like to reach a larger market of independent bookstores, you have a few options at this point, though we expect that marketing and distribution opportunities in this area will expand.

Independent Publishers Group, based in Chicago, is one of the largest distributors of books from independent publishers to independent bookstores. In some cases, IPG is willing to distribute self-published print books by single authors. John Blumenthal, author of *What's Wrong With Dorfman*, told us that when IPG agreed to list and distribute his self-published book, the result was a strong boost to his sales. IPG has recently inaugurated an e-book program that distributes e-books to independent booksellers in the same way that it distributes print books.

For further information, see the Independent Publisher's Group Web site at www.ipgbook.com, or call (312) 337-0747.

Another possibility is Booksite.com, which has recently made an alliance with Lightning Source, Inc., to provide e-book services to Booksite's network of independent booksellers.

One of Booksite's services to authors is PubLink (www.publink .net), a searchable database available to independents that provides information about publishers and authors. Authors can list their books and provide autobiographical data, pictures of themselves and other information, which is then readily accessible by all the members of Booksite's network.

For more information, see www.booksite.com, or call toll-free: 1-800-515-3322.

In Conclusion

As you can see, there are several distribution channels for your e-book. Certainly, the *most important* outlets are the major online booksellers. These operations have the financial clout to spend a lot of money bringing potential readers and buyers to their sites, and they have effective and well-designed facilities to let readers find your books.

The second most important outlet is your own Web site, if you have self-published your book, or your e-publisher's Web site, if an online house is publishing your work.

In the end, though, it doesn't matter *how* your e-book is distributed if readers don't know it is there. The many ways of letting them know and gaining their interest are called "marketing." The next chapters you'll read are devoted to a discussion of the many ways you can market and promote your e-book.

CHAPTER FORTY-ONE

THE IMPORTANCE OF MARKETING YOUR E-BOOK

According to even the lowest estimates, there are tens of millions of Web sites in existence, serving almost every conceivable purpose. The search engine Google (www.google.com) claims to search nearly 1.5 *billion* Web pages. If even .01 percent of them are involved in some sort of e-publishing endeavor, that means there are approximately 150,000 Web pages making e-books available. To make this number a bit more meaningful, consider that there are approximately 26,000 brick-and-mortar bookstores in the real world. In other words, there are about six times more e-book publishing sites on the Web than there are bookstores in the real world.

Now, try to imagine that you had to browse through all 26,000 bookstores in the real world to find something you might like to read. Pretty hard to do that, right?

Think how much harder it might be to look through hundreds of thousands, or even millions, of Web pages to find an author whose work you might like, but whom you've never heard of before.

In the real world, people find new authors by browsing bookstore shelves, seeing a cover that looks good or a title that sounds interesting in the section catering to their general preference—mystery, science fiction, memoir—and then picking up the book and reading the copy on the back cover or the first few paragraphs of the initial chapter. If everything looks good, they take the book to the counter, plunk down their money and take their purchase home.

Consider doing that with a million online Web sites. The short answer is: You can't. You can certainly use one of the Internet search engines like Yahoo or Google to track down books for sale online by authors you already know and like, but unfortunately, these search engines haven't yet reached the point where you can type in, "Find me books by authors that I might like well enough to think about buying." It just isn't possible—though it would be wonderful if it were.

Which brings us back to the notion of branded or gateway publishing. If you've bought and enjoyed books from a publisher in the past, you'll be more likely to at least consider books from the same publisher in the future, even if you know nothing about the author.

Although precise numbers are hard to come by, we can be reasonably certain there are hundreds of e-book publishers online and thousands of e-books available in one format or another.

Anybody who has much experience with the Internet and the World Wide Web these days understands that finding information is difficult, not because there is so little data to find, but instead because there is so much. Plug almost any word or phrase into a search engine, and you may get anything from hundreds of hits to hundreds of thousands.

This phenomenon is called "information overload," and it will only get worse as the Web itself grows by millions of pages every day. A search on the word "book" from google.com returns more than four million possibilities, and the word "e-books" gives you over three hundred thousand pages to take a look at. Obviously, nobody is going to look at hundreds of thousands or millions of Web pages just to track down your e-book.

So how can you make your e-books stand out in this screaming cacophony of information?

The Importance of Marketing Your E-Book

Well, luckily for all of us, there is a well-established body of knowledge on this question, knowledge honed in the real world for decades before it began to be adapted to the changing needs of the Internet and the digital revolution.

It's called marketing.

Marketing

Sometimes there seems to be as many definitions of this word as there are markets, so let's try to narrow it down a bit to suit our own purposes. For an e-publisher, marketing really means: *The entire process by which you create, distribute, advertise and promote your e-books in order to reach as many potential readers as possible.*

In previous chapters, we've discussed issues of creation and distribution. Now we will turn to the most commonly understood aspect of marketing: advertising and promotion.

Advertising and Promotion

Sometimes referred to as "A&P," this is a wide-ranging set of methods you can use to inform potential customers and readers why they should want your e-book, where they can find it and how they can obtain it.

If a tree falls in a forest and nobody hears it, is there a sound? If your e-book vanishes in a fog of thousands of Web pages so that nobody is aware that it exists, is there an e-book?

We're going to devote the next several chapters to a discussion about how you can make sure your own e-book doesn't disappear into the bottomless pit of information overload. We'll show you how to make your e-books stand out from the crowd and do so in such a compelling and attractive way that readers will flock to your writing.

CHAPTER FORTY-TWO

METHODS OF INTERNET/WEB PROMOTION TO AVOID

M.J. Rose, author of *In Fidelity, Lip Service* and *Private Places* (www.mjrose.com), is one of the most successful e-book authors in history. Along with her best-selling novels, she has also written a book with Angela Adair-Hoy, operator of the e-publishing house Booklocker (www.booklocker.com), called *How to Publish and Promote Online* (buy it at amazon.com: www.amazon.com/exec/obidos/ASIN/0312271913/qid=998372288/sr=1-1/ref=sc_b_1/104-4118264-4406330). This, by the way, is an excellent book by a pair of authors who've learned the secrets to successful e-publishing the hard way.

Rose and Adair-Hoy include in their book a chapter that details many of the Internet "blind alleys" that Ms. Rose was forced to deal with in her search for workable and effective ways to market her first e-book, *In Fidelity*.

Needle in a Haystack: Search Engines

Every once in a while you might receive a piece of e-mail or see a banner on a Web site offering to ensure your Web site is listed on dozens, even hundreds, of Internet search engines.

Now, at first glance, this may seem an attractive notion. The World Wide Web contains billions of individual Web pages. Most people use search engines like Yahoo, Google, Excite or AltaVista to look for pages containing something of specific interest to them. In fact, without search engines, it would be impossible to find anything in the chaotic jumble of the Web.

So, naturally, you'd probably think it's a good idea to make sure that whenever anybody comes looking for you, your Web page will pop up in most search engines. A few of the problems:

- Most of these offers to "list" you with hundreds of search pages want to charge you for the service, sometimes as much as a couple of hundred dollars.
- You don't need to be listed at hundreds or thousands of locations. Most Web surfers quickly find two or three search engines—usually among the largest—and use those almost exclusively.
- Most of the "pay-for-submission" services aren't really very effective—Ms. Rose discovered that, in one case, a service that promised to submit to four hundred engines for "only" $150 resulted in her page actually appearing on only ten search pages, and this meager result only after a wait of two weeks.
- Why pay for a service you can get for free?

The Solution—Free Submissions

There are several Web sites that offer "all-in-one" submissions to multiple search engines. All you have to do is fill out an online form one time, click a button and they will take it from there. Here is a good one:

Submit Express (www.submitexpress.com) offers free submission to more than forty of the largest search engines, including Google, Excite, Lycos, AltaVista and HotBot, as well as listings at "meta-search" pages (these "meta" engines search dozens of other search engines simultaneously).

If you're interested in learning how search engines work and how to improve your rankings on major search engines—getting your Web page into the first few returns on a search, an important factor to consider, given that most folks never read beyond the first few "hits" on a search page—you might want to visit Danny Sullivan's excellent Web site, Search Engine Watch (http://search enginewatch.com). Sullivan has written an extensive tutorial explaining the technology of search engines, along with tips on using them in the most effective way.

Check out Sullivan's *Search Engine Submission Tips* at http://search enginewatch.com/webmasters/index.html. Here you will learn tricks, tips and techniques about using HTML meta tags, keywords in page title design, page layout (search engines assign greater relevancy to text at the beginning of a page than at the end) and other methods that will increase your ranking in search engine presentations.

Buy Your Own: Commercial Mailing Lists

On the Internet, it sometimes seems that all everybody wants to do is sell you something. There are hundreds of sites that have compiled what are known as "opt-in" mailing lists, that is, lists of people who have signed up to receive e-mail on certain specific subjects.

The informative WilsonWeb Web Marketing Information Center offers a list of several *targeted direct e-mail list* purveyors, which they are careful to stipulate they have not personally investigated. However, your authors took a quick tour through the sites mentioned and found several willing to sell you a mailing list of people interested in the subject of books. One place we examined offered several such lists, ranging in price from $400 for 2,000 names to more than $3500 for a list of about 25,000 names.

M.J. Rose's experience with a similar service is instructive: At a cost of $1000, she purchased a list of 1,000 names. She tested several letters, picked the most effective and mailed it out. Final results? She sold ten copies of her book, a net return of 1 percent on her list—and a big-time net loss for her wallet.

Banner Ads

You've seen them, probably seen too many of them—those annoying little squares and rectangles that flutter or blink or pop up and get in the way of whatever you're really trying to see on some Web page you've visited.

They're called "banner ads." Once upon a time, they were going to be the "gold mine" of the World Wide Web and make multimillionaires out of the investors in every free content site known to man or woman.

Post-dot.com bust, we know it didn't happen. The reason is simple. The advertisers who were going to pay for all the prosperity discovered that banner advertising on the Web just wasn't very effective, and so they stopped doing it.

M.J. Rose discovered this same fact before a lot of other advertisers did. She paid to have a banner ad designed for her and then paid quite a bit more to buy space for the ad on several likely Web sites that catered to potential readers of her book.

After the dust had settled, Rose discovered she'd sold about five hundred books. That may sound like quite a bit, but in fact the return on her banner advertising investment was only a bit more than half of what she spent.

This sort of economics may have worked once upon a time for hundreds of aspiring dot.com businesses, but a quick glance at the stock market today makes it obvious this is no long-term recipe for success.

CHAPTER FORTY-THREE

MARKETING METHODS THAT WORK

D espite the disappointing experiences with some marketing methods we discussed in the last chapter, we do know of advertising and promotional techniques that do work and, even better, are either free or far less expensive than many of the more traditional approaches like commercial mailing lists or banner ads. These methods vary in both approach and the amount of old-fashioned elbow grease you'll have to apply, but in essence they boil down to one thing: good word of mouth.

People who make their living in the business of convincing you to buy goods and services have known for a long time that the best form of advertising you can possibly hope for is when your friend or neighbor—somebody you know and trust—tells you they tried a product and liked it.

But the Net isn't like your backyard, where the woman next door chats across the fence about the great barbecue grill she just found—or is it?

Our experience teaches us that in many ways the Internet and the Web are essentially the biggest backyard in human history.

So let's spend some time talking about how to get those digital backyard tongues wagging about *your* e-book. It might be easier than you think.

Your E-Book Marketing Plan

We know that if you've made it this far and have your e-book available in as many distribution channels as you can find, you're probably ready to rush right out and start yelling about it at the top of your digital lungs. Well, stop right there!

Unless you're one of those people who have a subconscious craving for personal disaster, the first thing you need to do is think. And what you need to think about is something the pros—those folks who've successfully sold everything from pet rocks to Cadillacs—call a "marketing plan."

When one of the huge national advertising agencies sets out to create a marketing plan for a product, the process can involve thousands of hours and millions of dollars. Before the first ad is placed, the first television commercial filmed or the first magazine photo shoot done, an enormous amount of time will be spent on surveys, focus groups, design conferences and just plain expensive brain-noodling. The end result of all this hard, high-priced labor will eventually be presented to the client in the form of a few typewritten pages bound in a nice leather cover with a title on the front: "Marketing Plan."

When you complete your own marketing process, you'll have a marketing plan just like the big guys, except yours will be tailored precisely to your own e-book. So put down that electronic megaphone, and let's get started.

Your marketing plan should include the following two elements:

- A concise description of that group of readers you believe will be interested in reading your book. This is your *market*.
- A strategy designed to make your market aware of the existence of your e-book and to convince them to obtain it. This is your *plan*.

Your Market

Before you start to think about your market, you need to think about your *product*. Your product is your e-book.

We know that may seem a cold and mercenary way to think about something over which you've sweated, bled and wept, but your potential readers don't know, and very likely don't care, about the effort you've put into your e-book's creation. What they are really interested in knowing, in advance if possible, is whether they can reasonably expect that their efforts to obtain your e-book will pay off—especially since there are thousands of other e-books available from which they can choose.

So spend some time thinking about your product, about your e-book. What is it? Is it long? Short? A steamy novel about the adventures of supermodels in exotic climes? A hard-hitting exposé of a horrid crime? A brisk and cheerful how-to book about breeding prize rabbits?

Would it be something a harried businessman might enjoy reading on his laptop while crammed into an economy seat between a wailing infant and a three-hundred-pound weightlifter? Or something a housewife might use to help her improve her floral arrangements?

If the last novel your best friend read was *Moby-Dick* in freshman literature thirty years ago, and since then he's read nothing but business books with titles like *Genghis's Mongol Secrets to Slaughter Your Way to the Top*, do you think he'd make a likely potential customer for your e-book romance novel *Passionate Sighs*?

Once you've critically and dispassionately decided what kind of e-book you've written, you've taken a giant step toward discovering the sort of reader who might enjoy reading it. And that knowledge will have a huge impact on the strategies you design to let that potential reader know about your e-book.

After deciding what sort of readers are part of your potential market, you may be wondering how to go about finding these people. Demographics can provide part of the answer.

Demographic Research

Demographic research deals with the study of human groups: size, growth, distribution and other characteristics—such as reading preferences. Think of Internet demographics as a map that defines the type and location of your potential customers on the World Wide Web. The better your "map," the easier and more effective will be your efforts to target your desired customer group.

Now, to be sure, solid studies of the demographics of the Internet and the World Wide Web are still in their infancy, expensive and hard to come by. Worse yet, the demographics of the Web are changing and growing so rapidly, today's studies may be outmoded and inaccurate as soon as tomorrow.

Still, there are potentially helpful resources out there. One of the best we've found is the Web Marketing and E-Commerce Center, maintained by Dr. Ralph F. Wilson, at www.wilsonweb.com. This excellent site has a section devoted to Web demographics at www .wilsonweb.com/webmarket/demograf.htm.

Here you can find a host of articles and demographic data about the people who use the Web—your potential customers! If you want to spend a little money, you can buy an annual subscription to Dr. Wilson's online magazine, *Web Commerce Today*, for $49.95. Not only is the monthly magazine an excellent information source itself, but subscribers have full access to a database of more than eight thousand articles, surveys and studies at the site.

This site is a treasure trove of information and advice for Web marketers of every stripe, from the most inexperienced beginner to the sophisticated pro. We do recommend that you subscribe to the magazine, if only to get full access to the database. There is really no other source of Web marketing data as extensive and authoritative available on the Web today.

Use this information to discover the locations, habits, purchasing preferences and other valuable attributes of your potential reading audience. It will be of critical importance in devising methods to reach and sell to your market.

Do-It-Yourself Demographics

Another way to get a general idea of what sort of people read various kinds of books is to try to discover who reads books that are similar to yours. One good way of doing this makes use of the Internet.

One of the oldest components of the Internet—it was around long before the Web made its appearance and is still going strong— is called *Usenet*, or, more commonly, *the newsgroups*.

There are currently more than fifty thousand newsgroups covering almost every conceivable topic. Think of a newsgroup as a kind of electronic kaffeeklatsch where folks gather to discuss a single subject of interest.

You can access newsgroups as long as you have an Internet connection and a piece of software called a *newsreader*. There are dozens of newsreaders—one is included free with Windows Internet Explorer, called "Outlook Express," and the Netscape browser also includes a free newsreading program. Another good newsreader is Agent (www.forteinc.com/agent/index.htm), which costs $29, but also offers a free version called Free Agent.

Once you've got your newsreader up and running, look for newsgroups dedicated to an author whose work is similar to your own. For instance, if you write horror fiction, you might check out alt .books.stephen-king. We just did and found nearly ten thousand messages posted by fans who wanted to talk about the master of scary writing.

Now, most of you won't want to read all ten thousand messages—that would take longer than reading all of King's novels!

Marketing Methods That Work

However, you could skim through the postings to make a generalized estimate of the sort of people who do read King's work and are excited enough about it to join an online discussion group to discuss it. Those same types of people may be interested in your horror writing as well.

When we skimmed through the posting in King's newsgroup, it was readily apparent that the large majority of posters were male. Sampling several posts showed that the male posters seemed to fall into two age groups—20 to 30 and over 50. This is valuable information for you as an e-book marketer. These two groups could well be the market for your horror novel, too.

Your Marketing Worksheet

Once you've done some hard thinking about what you've written and some research to find some groups of potential readers for your type of writing, you can begin to put together your *marketing worksheet.*

The first section might look something like this:

MARKETING WORKSHEET

E-book Title: DARK BLOOD

Type: Fiction

Genre: Horror

Primary Characteristics: Fast-paced, bloody, violent.

Secondary Characteristics: Adapted from a series of mysterious murders that took place in Chicago in the late 1950s. Settings are historically accurate.

Potential Markets:

- Horror fans.
- Male readers between the ages of 20–30 and over 50.
- Female readers 30–50. (You discover this is a sizable group

from examining the King newsgroup.)

- Readers in the Chicago area who might be interested in the historical aspects of the fictional account.

Once you've reached this point, you'll find that you've taken a large step toward understanding the basic outlines of what your most important marketing task will be: letting your potential market know about your book and convincing them to buy it.

There are several methods of doing so that are easily within the reach of even the newest e-publisher. In the next chapters, we'll show you how to identify and use those methods that are best for you.

CHAPTER FORTY-FOUR

E-MAIL SIGNATURES: ONE SIMPLE THING YOU CAN DO TO MARKET YOUR E-BOOK

Not everyone has the sort of marketing budget available to the folks who sell Chevrolets or Nikes. In fact, hardly anyone does, and that probably includes you. So what can you do to sell your e-book that costs little or nothing?

Quite a bit, actually. In this chapter, we discuss one of the simplest—your e-mail signature. If you do nothing else to market your book, at least consider following our advice for this important way to reach readers.

Your E-Mail Signature

Sometime in the past few years, the number of e-mails sent across the Internet exceeded the number of telephone calls made across standard phone lines. We checked our own e-mail habits for the last year and discovered that we'd sent out more than two thousand of the darned things. You've probably sent a few e-mails yourself, in fact. At the bottom of your e-mail, you can place your *signature*. It could be something as simple as your name, or it could be as elaborate as dozens of lines of boilerplate. In either case, your signature is viewed by everyone who receives an e-mail from you.

Recall the Usenet newsgroups we just discussed. Newsgroups are really nothing more than collections of individual e-mails but are posted in such a way that all members of the newsgroup can read them. This is an even better form of exposure for your e-mail signature than private e-mail, which is only read by the person you send it to. Posted on a newsgroup, your e-mail signature might be read by hundreds, even thousands of fellow newsreaders. So what better place can you think of to let people know that you've written an e-book they might like to read?

In the case of e-mail signatures, more is definitely not better. In the first place, there is a bit of long-standing Internet etiquette (often called "netiquette") that cautions that an e-mail signature should not be longer than four lines. With some Internet veterans, this stricture is so ingrained that not only will they not look at long signatures, they won't even read e-mails with long signatures. So what can you do in four lines or less to market your book? Quite a bit, actually.

The first thing you need to do is announce that you've written an e-book (or e-books). Use the first line of your signature for this. It might look something like: "Melody Anywriter, author of *Green Grow the Snails in the Garden of Love.*"

The next line should include the most powerful tool available on the Internet, a URL *link* to a Web page. This link should take the form: www.someplace.com/booklinkwhatever.html.

This sort of link will be interpreted by most e-mail and news-readers as a *clickable link*, that is, all the reader needs to do is click on that link to be immediately transported to the page linked to. So what should you link to?

You have two basic choices: either a page where the reader can buy your book or a page where she can learn more about your book. If your book is listed at Amazon.com or BarnesandNoble.com, for instance, you might put a link to the Amazon page that sells the book and provides information about it, as well. If you are selling your book primarily from your own Web site, you would link to that instead. Or if your book is being distributed by your e-publisher, that is where you would direct your reader.

Here are some real-life samples of e-mail signatures. Fred Willard, a much applauded mystery author, signs his e-mails like this:

"Fred Willard, author of *Down on Ponce* &
Princess Naughty and the Voodoo Cadillac
http://personal.atl.bellsouth.net/~fwillard"

Willard has linked to his personal home page, where potential readers can find out more about the two books he lists in his signature.

Author Kate Saundby does it this way:

"Freddie aka Kate Saundby
shippard@wk.net   www.nublis.com
A CIRCLE OF ARCS ISBN 158338-468-5"

This link is to the Web page of the e-publisher who distributes Saundby's e-book, *A Circle of Arcs.* Clicking on it in an e-mail program will take readers directly to a place where they can learn more about the book and even buy it.

Unless you have a host of books to market, you've only used up two or three lines of your four-line signature. Is there anything else you can add that might be helpful? Well, what about a line from a favorable review? If somebody has said something nice about your e-book, that sort of compliment can carry a good deal of weight with potential readers, just as readers are more likely to consider a book somebody has told them they liked. So if you can find a line like "a blockbuster debut" or "the new John Grisham" in a review of your book, feel free to add that to your signature. After all, it's your signature. You can put whatever you want in there.

Don't have any reviews yet? Don't worry. We'll tell you how to generate them in the next chapter.

CHAPTER FORTY-FIVE

HOW TO GET YOUR E-BOOK REVIEWED

R eviews are important to an author. Good reviews from an established, respected source with a wide distribution like *The New York Times* or *The New Yorker* can send sales of a book soaring. Bad reviews are a slightly different story.

Somebody once said that the only bad kind of publicity was *no* publicity, but we doubt if you'd want to post an excerpt from a review of your e-book that begins: "I hated this book!"

And, to be brutally honest, there may be some readers who feel that way. Even worse, some of them may write reviews that say so. First, you know not to take these sorts of things seriously, right? The truth is, you can't please everybody. Authors from Homer to Shakespeare to Danielle Steele have all gotten ripped by the peanut gallery on occasion. No matter how wonderful your own e-book is, some readers will react to it with an abrupt case of hives and the urge to institute a public book burning. You can't really burn an e-book, but you can "flame" it. "Flaming" is the art of public insult on the Internet, especially in Usenet newsgroups.

But we'll tell you a little secret. Just as there will always be somebody who hates your book, there will always be somebody who thinks it is the finest piece of literature produced since Dante penned his little travelogue about his journey through Hell.

The trick is to find someone who has expressed these pleasing sentiments publicly. Here are a few dos and don'ts about the process of doing so.

Find Your Dream Review

Established Review Sources

There are thousands of long-established forums for the review of literature, ranging from your local newspaper to *The New York Times Review of Books*. Many of these reviewers have been somewhat reluctant to consider reviewing e-books, but that lamentable situation is slowly changing.

Publishers Weekly ran its first review of an e-book, Dick Adler's *The Mozart Code*, in May 1999. Since that time, they have reviewed several more e-books, including M.J. Rose and Angela Adair-Hoy's *How to Publish and Promote Online*, their first review of a nonfiction e-book, as well as Stephen King's landmark e-book, *Riding the Bullet*. *PW*, as it is known in the industry, also now accepts book galleys in digital format for review. Jeff Zaleski, head of *PW*'s Forecasts Department, often reviews e-books for this trade journal. E-mail him at e-forecasts@cahners.com for further information and the current policy regarding e-book reviews at *Publishers Weekly*.

Science Fiction

If you've written something in the science fiction genre, there are several established review venues open to you.

Locus Magazine is a highly influential journal of news and reviews in the science fiction world. Their office states that they are open to reviewing e-books "if one of our reviewers finds something they want to review." Submit your science fiction or fantasy e-book to *Locus* via e-mail to http://locus@locusmag.com, with "Attention:

Reviews" in your subject line. *Locus* also reviews print-on-demand books. Mail a copy of your book to: Locus Publications, P.O. Box 13305, Oakland CA 94661.

Analog Science Fiction and Fact is the oldest science fiction magazine currently extant. Its staff reviewer, Tom Easton, has in the past reviewed e-books, and we've been told that the magazine's review policy is the same for e-books and print books: "If we like it, we may review it." *Analog*'s e-book submission policy is slightly different than *Locus*'s, however. They prefer to receive e-mail containing a link to a Web page version of the book, rather than having the entire file attached to the e-mail. Send submissions for review to analog@dellmagazines.com.

o o o

The world of book reviewing, just like the digital world of e-books, is in a constant state of flux. Many reviewers who wouldn't even consider e-books are now reviewing them. The best way to find out if a forum will consider your e-book is simply to ask.

Online E-Book Reviews

Naturally, online venues—e-zines, literary Web sites and other outposts of the digital nation—are much more open to reviewing e-books, though, in general, such sites are not as well known or established as the more traditional print reviewers. Nonetheless, a good review is a good review; so you should make the effort to offer your e-book for review to as many of these Web sites as you can manage.

Luckily, by the very nature of the Web, this is easier to do than with standard print outlets. The biggest advantage to you as an author is the ability to submit your work in digital format, either via e-mail or as a link to a Web version of the work. This means you can present your work to three hundred different reviewers almost as easily as to one.

However, you should do a bit of homework first. Simply plugging the phrase "e-book reviews" into a search engine like google .com returns several hundred results. Certainly not all of these "hits" will be interested in reviewing your book. There are also many other potential online review sources, information about which we'll list shortly.

Carefully go through these resources. Visit the Web pages. Read the submission instructions and follow them. Don't make the mistake of sending your e-book romance of tender, endless love to a site that reviews only business consulting books.

As a general rule, there are many, many examples of almost everything on the World Wide Web. This includes Web sites that review e-books. Do the same sort of research in selecting the proper venues for your e-book reviews as you would in searching out a publisher or an agent for a print book. An unthinking, unresearched "scattershot" approach to finding online reviewers is not only time-consuming and wasteful, it is just plain rude.

EBook Connections (www.ebookconnections.com), an online site, does reviews for an established and highly respected print publication, the *Midwest Book Review*. They offer reviews in all genres.

EBook Connections details their review policy at www.ebookcon nections.com/reviews/submissionguidelines.htm.

An excerpt: "Send queries to http://reviews@ebookconnections .com and include title, author, publisher, publication date, genre/ subgenre, approximate number of words or pages, ISBNs, formats available and prices, short book summary and author bio. If we are considering your book, we'll e-mail for a copy (Rocket eBook compatible format). Alternatively, you can send a CD, diskette, print ARCs, galleys or books to: Jamie Engle, eBook Connections, P.O. Box 850296, Richardson, TX, 75085-0296."

eBook Connections also does extensive original reviews of

e-books that are offered at their Web site.

eBook Connections maintains an excellent and up-to-date collection of links to other e-book review venues and includes with each listing a summary of the sorts of e-books each site reviews.

Find the list here: www.ebookconnections.com/readerconnecti ons/book_review_sites.htm.

ePublishing Connections (www.epublishingconnections.com), sister site to eBook Connections, also offers a list of links, similarly annotated, to online e-book reviewers.

Find the list here: www.epublishingconnections.com/book_revi ews.htm.

Vox Populi: Readers Review E-Books

Trust us. Some reader out there will like your e-book. And readers are often voluble about the books they like. Just as those who hate your e-book may be not at all shy about saying so, those who like it will often make their approval known as well.

All of the major online booksellers offer a mechanism by which readers can post their opinions about books. These reader reviews (or at least links to them) appear on the same page the book itself is listed on. Even better, quite often such reviews are as well written and well thought out as anything done by professional reviewers.

As an example, one of your authors garnered this review from a page for one of his books at Amazon.com:

"I won't do Mr. Quick the injustice of comparing him to anyone else in the Sci-Fi world. He truly stands alone. His books are somewhat hard to come by but may be republished in the future. If you like Niven, Pournelle or Stephenson you'll love all of Quick's work . . ."

Another source of reader reviews is the online e-publishers themselves. Many e-books are not listed in the catalogs of the large online booksellers but are instead marketed solely through e-publishers' Web sites or through the Web site of the author her-self. More than a few e-publisher Web sites allow readers to contrib-ute reviews of the e-books they publish. If your e-book is distributed through such a site, make sure you check the review section on a regular basis.

Note to self-e-publishers: Make sure you provide some way for readers to offer feedback about your e-book on your Web site. You may be surprised at the wonderful reviews you garner. And your authors may find they appreciate the feedback as well, insofar as it gives them clues about reader acceptance of their own writing.

Trimming the "Fat": Quoting From Reviews

How many times have we all seen a movie reviewer open a diatribe thusly:

> This exercise in wretched film excess is so awful it's fasci-nating, like watching a train crash in progress. The film is a brilliant example of the perils of offering money, cameras, and free will to a director whose talents barely exceed those of cockroaches. This movie tries to be a roller-coaster thriller ride when, in fact, it is a three-way collision among utterly talentless actors, a deranged director and a writer who evi-dently types his best work with his feet. If you want to know far more than necessary about how not to make a movie, go see this one.
>
> —Big Time Reviewer

By the time the studio publicity department finishes "trimming the review for length," it reads:

> Fascinating . . . brilliant. A roller-coaster thriller ride . . . Go see this one!
>
> —Big Time Reviewer

How to Get Your E-Book Reviewed

OK. We won't advocate surgery quite this radical on your own e-book reviews, but a bit of literary snip-and-tuck, if kept reasonably honest, is not beyond the ethical bounds.

For instance, one of the authors of this book has an e-book currently listed at both bn.com and Amazon.com.

At Amazon, a reader has posted this review of the book:

"I've been trying to go through whatever anybody says is cyberpunk and have come across some horrible books. This one isn't half bad. It's got some good twists and the ending is something unexpected. If you like cyberpunk novels, I'd add this to your list."

Not exactly stand-up-and-cheer, right? But not really bad, either. And without utterly sacrificing the intent of the reviewer, the review can be quoted thusly without damning yourself to eternal fire:

"Good twists, and the ending is something unexpected. If you like cyberpunk novels . . . add this to your list."

Sounds better, doesn't it? And this version has the added attraction of being just the right length to fit neatly onto your e-mail signature.

Reviews in a Nutshell

To sum things up, thanks to a combination of established, traditional review sources and the review opportunities opened up by the digital revolution, there may be thousands of sources out there for good reviews for your e-book. Make use of the methods and possibilities we've just discussed to find those reviews.

And once you have, what then? The next chapter describes how you can use reviews as part of your plan to market and promote your e-book.

CHAPTER FORTY-SIX

FOCUSING ON YOUR POTENTIAL MARKET

R emember that marketing worksheet we started? It went like this:

E-book Title: DARK BLOOD
Type: Fiction
Genre: Horror
Primary Characteristics: Fast-paced, bloody, violent.
Secondary Characteristics: Adapted from a series of mysterious murders that took place in Chicago in the late 1950s. Settings are historically accurate.

Potential Markets
- Horror fans.
- Male readers between the ages of 20–30 and over 50.
- Female readers 30–50. (You discover this is a sizable group from examining the King newsgroup.)
- Readers in the Chicago area who might be interested in the historical aspects of the fictional account.

Let's get started on the all-important second section now.

You start with the header: Advertising and Promotion. Beneath that heading, you put: E-Mail Signature.

You then list the e-mail signature you've created, making use of an excerpt from a particularly kind review you located:

Frank E. Writer, author of DARK BLOOD
"Scared the peepers right out of my skull."—review at Amazon.com.

Then you add a URL link to the page at Amazon that contains the review and, not so coincidentally, your e-book, available for immediate purchase:

www.amazon.com/anybook/anywhere/gothere

Now remember: Your e-mail signature is an advertising tool. You can set your e-mail and newsreader programs to automatically add it to every e-mail and newspost you send out. Check the "help" on your own e-mail program to find out how to do this.

As we said earlier, there is no realistic, cost-effective way you can reach all of the four hundred million Internet users in any meaningful way. So we narrowed down the potential market in the first section of your marketing plan.

Your next challenge is discovering just how to reach that smaller group. First, let's discuss one marketing plan *not* to do.

Spam: Why to Avoid This Marketing Method

"Spam" is used as a general term for "unsolicited e-mail." Spam has a long and dishonorable history on the Internet. Oddly enough, the term is not directly borrowed from the name of the famous canned luncheon meat. Those who've looked into the matter believe it came from a famous Monty Python sketch that featured uncontrollable floods of SPAM luncheon meat as the point of the joke.

In any event, nothing gets peoples' dander up like spam. If you've been on the Net for any time at all, you've no doubt received e-mails from hosts of senders about things you have no interest in at all—or even e-mails that cause active revulsion, such as invitations to various pornographic sites. You wonder how and why these people send such things to you. You certainly didn't ask them to. All this stuff is unsolicited e-mail. It is spam.

Strangely enough, there is a lot of spam going around that offers to sell you software programs that will let you do some spamming yourself. "Thirty-five million e-mail addresses!" says one. "Sell to everybody on the World Wide Web!" trumpets another.

You think, "Hmmm . . . " And you wonder what would happen if even one hundredth of one percent of those thirty-five million people bought your e-book. After all, thirty-five hundred people at, say, seven dollars per book. Why that would be . . .

Please. Don't think that way.

In the first place, spam is terribly wasteful, and in the second, it is downright rude. Do *you* like receiving those dozens of automatic e-mail ads for "Make Money Fast" schemes in your e-mail box every day? Would you want your own good author's name to be associated with a similar method of "promotion"?

But if that isn't enough to dissuade you, spamming is a practice outlawed in just about every Internet service provider's "Terms of Service." You didn't read all that tiny boilerplate you received when you signed up for Internet service? You should have. Spamming is one of the quickest ways to get your account cancelled you can imagine. And once your account is cancelled, your carefully designed Web site vanishes into the ether right along with it.

And make no mistake: If you do spam, you will be discovered. Somebody will complain to your ISP, and that will be the end of that—and a good part of your e-book marketing effort as well.

Focusing on Your Potential Market

Flavors of Spam

There are two kinds of spam: e-mail spamming and Usenet news-group spamming. Either one can get your ISP account yanked, but they differ somewhat.

We've already talked about e-mail spam. That's the stuff that's sent out in bulk to thousands or millions of unsuspecting victims. Think of it the same way you think about all that junk mail that clogs your real-world mailbox every day.

On the Usenet newsgroups, there is a variation on this bulk-mail ploy that involves sending the same message to thousands of different newsgroups, almost all of which are talking about some subject that has nothing to do with the content of the bulk mail.

For instance, the folks in alt.children.potty-training would have no interest in learning that you've written an e-book called *Sixty Days to Perfect Eyelashes*. On the other hand, they might well be interested in a book titled *Sixty Days to Perfect Potty-Training*, a difference we'll be discussing shortly.

The second form of newsgroup spamming involves posting the same message over and over to a single or a few newsgroups. The message may seem to be on-topic—an ad for a book about potty training posted on a newsgroup discussing potty training—but posting the same message several times a day, interminably, on that group is spam, and it will make you far more enemies than friends.

So how often is permissible? Once a month might be OK. Certainly no more than once a week, and if you *do* use the shorter timetable, expect to receive a lot of heat from at least some members of the group in question.

○ ○ ○

OK, now you know what *not* to do. But one of the best features of the Internet, from a promotional point of view, is that it allows you to reach out to large numbers of people quickly and, even more important, cheaply.

So how can you take advantage of this feature of the digital revolution without either angering hordes of people or losing your connection to the Internet entirely?

We are now focusing on narrowing your potential market, not expanding it. At this point, quite frankly, you want to start small, with the idea being that once you've begun to effectively reach a small market, you can then expand from that base.

And there are ways you can accomplish this using both e-mail and the Usenet newsgroups. For a discussion of these ways, see the next chapter.

CHAPTER FORTY-SEVEN

USING E-MAIL ANNOUNCEMENTS TO ADVERTISE AND PROMOTE YOUR E-BOOK

I n order to promote your e-book through e-mail, you need to have an announcement first. Think of your announcement as a news release, keeping in mind that it must perform one main function as well as possible: *Make the recipient want to learn more.*

So let's take a small diversion and discuss how to write a "grabber" e-mail release about your e-book.

The first thing you should do is spend a little time thinking about the predigital world and the way you bought—and probably still do buy—print books. As you wander the aisles of your favorite bookstore, what are the aspects of a book that catch your attention and raise your interest level?

The first detail is probably location. If you're interested in horror novels, you probably go to the shelves that are stocked with those kinds of books. Perhaps you have a few favorite authors, and your first step is to check the shelves for anything new from them.

Once you've done that, perhaps you look around for something new and interesting. The first thing that grabs your eye is some books that are turned face-outward on the shelf so you can easily see their covers.

Lots of bright colors with titles are printed in shiny foil, the same kind of glittery stuff that attracts crows and pack rats. Usually the titles are bigger than the names of the authors—most of whom you don't recognize anyway—so you look a little harder.

Hmmm. *The Thrilling Adventures of Darian Brown, Psychic Sleuth.* Nope. That one doesn't do anything for you. You pass by, still reading, until you spot: *Dark Blood.*

Hmmm, again. Short and punchy. Sounds kind of interesting.

You take down the book and look more closely at the cover. The author's name is unfamiliar, but right beneath it is this:

"The greatest thing since sliced brains . . ."—Stephen King.

Aha! You may not know the great horror-maestro personally, but after reading every one of the twelve million words he's had published, you sure feel like he's a friend of yours. Maybe even a neighbor. And evidently he likes this book.

You flip it over and take a look at the back cover. There's a blurb there, a synopsis of the book in a few sentences:

"One morning Sandy Smith wakes up from a nightmare to find a severed head in his garbage can. Within a few short days, Smith's sleepy Chicago neighborhood of Pinewood is convulsed by horror, as three more dismembered corpses appear, surrounded by mysterious hieroglyphs written in blood—and Smith's own name!

"As his dreams grow worse, Smith wonders if he's awakened from a nightmare or entered one in the real world. And while the police search for a grisly serial killer, Smith slowly realizes that he's faced with something even more terrifying: a dark and bloody secret from beyond the grave . . ."

Now *hey*, you think. This sounds pretty good. And I grew up in Chicago, just a few streets over from Pinewood. In fact, I seem to remember something I heard about, something weird that happened a long time ago . . .

Using E-Mail Announcements to Advertise and Promote Your E-Book

Five minutes later you're plunking the book down at the cash register and fishing for your wallet.

That's the process you want to think about when you write a grabber of an e-mail about your e-book.

Putting the Pieces Together

Location

In this case, "location" doesn't mean where you find the book, it means where you send your e-mails. You wouldn't look for a horror novel in the Christian Living section; by the same token, you don't send information about *Dark Blood* to a Web site called yournewba by.com.

Finding the Right Location

Your book is a horror novel, dark, bloody, violent. If you had to sum up its genre in a couple of words, you'd probably say, "Dark horror."

Well and good. Plug those two words into a search engine. We did so, and came up with 186,000 "hits," or pages that have some sort of relationship to those two words.

Now, obviously, you can't check through 186,000 Web pages. And it's not necessary that you do. One of the characteristics of most search engines is that the deeper you get into their lists, the less connection the results have to the original search entry. You should, however, read through the summaries of the first five hundred results. If you're really dedicated, check the first thousand. If you find something that looks like an interesting possibility, click on the link to the site. You do this for two reasons: first, to see if the Web site actually exists; second, to see if the site is what the search summary says it is.

Examples: On our search, the first result was a Web site called "DarkEcho Horror." The summary sounded like a strong possibility, so we clicked on over for a visit. The place turned out to be dedicated to horror in all its forms, including movies and books. And—how convenient—DarkEcho Horror does book reviews!

Put any such Web site you find on your list of potential markets for your book. If you go through five hundred hits from a decent search engine, you can expect at least 20 percent of those results to be good possibilities for you, no matter what sort of book you've written. So five hundred results ought to yield a hundred good possibilities, and a thousand should give you two hundred.

When you complete this process, you've made a giant leap toward finding your location. You've found a place where folks hang out who might very well be looking for a book just like the one you've written.

Covers: The "Front" of Your E-Mail

What's the first thing anybody sees when they open up their e-mail reader and see that "they've got mail"?

It's called a *subject line*. It's the equivalent of the "cover" of your e-mail promotion, and it may be the only shot you'll get at convincing the receiver to read further. Be sure your subject line does the job you want it to.

Press and release: Thanks to the wonders of modern spam, even the most obscure Web sites manage to get on hundreds of automated commercial mailing lists. Quite often, the subject line of such e-mails will begin with "Press Release: Read Immediately!" And quite often, such e-mails will be deleted unread, either by the irritated recipient or by an automatic deletion feature of the e-mail program itself.

On the other hand, while vague chattiness along the lines of "Hi, how are you today" may not get you the digital guillotine immediately, it may get your e-mail shunted to the "read later—a lot later" folder.

You don't want to be deleted or shunted. Either one can be painful. So you want to make sure your "cover" subject line contributes to rather than hinders your chances of having your e-mail read.

Be businesslike. Ideally, you'd like the Web sites you query to review your e-book or, failing that, at least mention its existence. Say so up front: "Request for review." This opening at least tells the recipient there is some legitimate business afoot.

Follow that opening with a colon, and then explain what the review request refers to. "Request for review: *Dark Blood,* a horror novel."

This may not have the same grabber potential as "You've inherited ten million dollars," but it will at least get your e-mail put into the "read" folder, and that's what you want.

The Heart of the Matter

Open With Kind Words

The body of your e-mail should start with that review excerpt we talked about earlier. Wait a minute! Aren't we asking for a review right now?

Sure. But if your book is already up on your Web site or on your e-publisher's Web site or one of the big online bookstores, somebody has probably already said something nice about it. Here's your chance to use it. It's sort of like using little fish as bait for bigger fish. Of course, if the reader who posts a nice review on Amazon.com does happen to be Stephen King . . .

Back to business. Don't beat around the bush. Open with your request. "Would you consider reviewing my e-book horror novel, *Dark Blood?*"

Then hit them with the review excerpts.

"Readers at Amazon.com said, 'Great . . . thrilling . . . scared the freckles right off my face . . .' "

Follow this with your carefully crafted synopsis of three to five pages: "One morning Sandy Smith wakes up . . ."

Ask and Ye Shall Receive: The Clincher

Once your synopsis is done, you've pretty much taken your best shot. All that remains is to get specific about what you want from the reader of your e-mail.

Be businesslike. Don't plead. Something along the lines of: "If *Dark Blood* sounds like your cup of gore, I'd be happy to either send you a copy on disk or as an e-mail attachment. The book is in .txt, .lit, .pdf and .html formats. It is also online for review purposes at www.myplace.com/darkblood/reviewers.html.

Finish with a standard sort of business letter finale: "Thank you very much for your time. I look forward to hearing from you."

And that's it.

Send your e-mail to your mailing list and wait for the rave reviews—or at least the favorable mentions—to roll in. Follow up if you hear nothing after six weeks.

Mailing list? But I thought you said . . .

Nope. We said *commercial* mailing list. But that list you made from grinding your way through all those search engine results? That's a mailing list too. And a better one than you could buy because you've tailored it precisely to the market you want to reach.

CHAPTER FORTY-EIGHT

PROMOTING YOUR E-BOOK THROUGH ELECTRONIC BULLETIN BOARDS

It's a little hard for those who don't participate in newsgroups on the Internet to understand the purposes they serve. While the basic description of a Usenet newsgroup as *an electronic bulletin board where people post e-mails that discuss a common interest* is technically accurate, it bears about as much relation to what really goes on as does describing the United Nations as an "international political gabfest."

It's been estimated that between 10 and 15 percent of all Internet users participate in newsgroups, which means thirty to fifty million people read and/or post to Usenet. You can't reach all of them. In fact, you don't want to reach all of them—just the ones you can reasonably expect to be interested in your e-book.

Usenet Culture

How can an electronic bulletin board have a culture? The same way any group of people with similar interests can. Your family has a culture, a way of doing things, doesn't it? So does your hometown, even your country. Usenet groups are no different. With more than fifty thousand of them—and the number grows every day—the global culture of Usenet is made up of many thousands of smaller cultures. The reason for this is the way Usenet grows.

Whenever some readers of any single group begin to feel that the group no longer addresses their needs or interests, they often split away from the original group and form a new one that's more to their liking because it is different from the group they left.

On the subject of writing, for instance: The original group on Usenet that concerned writing and writers was called "misc.writing."

Usenet is divided into several general categories called "hierarchies." The "comp" groups deal with all things computer, for instance. "Sci" are groups organized around scientific discussions. "Talk" groups, well, they're interested in talking about something, generally in the form of debates that sometimes become quite heated. When the heat gets high enough, it's called "flaming," which is the tactic of insult and an art form all to itself.

"Misc" deals with the vaguely nebulous "miscellaneous" category, discussions that don't quite fit into any other categories. Misc .writing was originally charted to discuss anything and everything about writing.

A final category is called "alt," for "alternate." This is a free-for-all. There are no rules for creating alt groups, and as a consequence this is by far the largest category of all newsgroups.

Over misc.writing's history, it began to fragment somewhat because subsets of its readers came to feel the group did not properly address their specific writing needs. So, misc.writing.screenplays was the first to split away so the screenwriters could have their own discussion group. Several others later appeared, covering topics like technical writing, poetry and science fiction. Finally alt.writing was created by folks who felt misc.writing was just too limited for their interest. There are probably now a couple of dozen groups focused primarily on writing, and maybe others that don't have the word "writing" in their names, but talk mostly about it anyway.

Many people interested in writing follow more than one group because each group is different, not just in topic matter, but in the culture of the group itself. Misc.writing, for instance, does talk about the specifics of writing, but it has become much like a "cocktail party" for writers, who talk about everything under the sun. Misc.screenwriting is more focused on the topic of screenwriting but often launches extended discussions of film criticism in general. Alt.writing is known for extremely vitriolic discussions; "flame wars" often spring up, which can be somewhat shocking to the uninitiated—especially if new members find themselves the target of flamers.

Something else you should know about newsgroups: Far more people "lurk" than "post." *Lurkers* are members who only read but never post their own comments. Most veteran Usenet users believe that lurkers outnumber posters by close to a hundred to one, although by their very nature, lurkers (they lurk, after all) are hard to count. If this estimate is close to being accurate, it would mean that misc.writing, which averages about five hundred regular posters, is actually read by nearly fifty thousand. That's a lot of potential readers to find in one place.

Needles in the Haystack: Finding the Right Newsgroups

Your newsreading program will generally provide you a way to search by name for specific newsgroups. Let's return to *Dark Blood*, our e-book horror novel.

Plugging the word "horror" into Microsoft Outlook Express returns the names of nearly two dozen groups that discuss something that relates to horror. Now, this isn't an enormous number of groups, and you could probably glance through all of them in a reasonable amount of time in order to determine the most likely candidates.

But recall that when you began to put your marketing plan together, you developed a few potential markets that weren't necessarily only horror fans. What about those who might be interested in the Chicago historical aspect of your book? There are a dozen groups with "chicago" in their name, and while most of them don't look likely, you might read it for other reasons. On the other hand, "history" returns dozens of newsgroups, several of which look like good possibilities. In general, you'll just have to do the grunt work of reading some of them in order to find the right ones.

Culture Clash: Making Your Entrance to Usenet

Probably the first step a writer promoting her book thinks when she first discovers Usenet is: "Great! I'll just post something about my e-book horror novel right away to every horror group I can find."

Wrong.

Of course, you *can* do that, but unless you like being on the receiving end of an avalanche of insulting posts from every flamer on the group, it would be a mistake.

You wouldn't leave your hometown in Illinois, travel to Paris, enter the first bar you find, and demand that everybody look at the pictures of your vacation in the Wisconsin dairylands, would you? Well, maybe you would, but you'd be braver than we are.

Most sane folks, when they find themselves a stranger in a strange land, use a bit of common sense. They keep their mouths shut and try to soak up as much of the local customs and language as they can before they start chatting with the natives. The more prepared tourists even read a guidebook or two and check out some maps of the territory.

You'll want to follow similar steps with Usenet. Once you find some likely groups, go ahead and lurk. Start reading the posts, but resist the urge to reply immediately. It's hard to do sometimes, but control yourself.

Many newsgroups maintain both *charters* and *FAQs*. Charters contain the reason the group was created in the first place and may include some rules for posting the original creators set up: For instance, misc.writing does not permit readers to post their own writing to the group.

Usually the charter will either be posted regularly or a link to it will be posted. FAQs—frequently asked questions—are an even better source of information about a newsgroup. They tend to be changed to reflect any changes in the group and are often updated to reflect real questions. Whenever a particular question becomes very common on the group, the FAQ maintainer will add the answer to the FAQ.

You can find group FAQs posted on the groups themselves, usually on a regular basis, or you can find thousands of them archived in various locations. A good place to start is the huge set of Usenet group FAQs maintained at the Internet FAQ Archive (www.faqs.org/faqs/).

The Lay of the Land: Reading Usenet for Fun and Profit

When you first log on to a newsgroup with your newsreader program, it will download "unread messages" to your machine so you can read them. These messages are downloaded from *news servers*, special computers designed to distribute news messages. Because of the tremendous total number of all Usenet messages, older ones are generally erased from these servers. With a busy newsgroup like misc.writing, your initial download will probably not show any messages older than a month or so—and even that total will amount to several thousand individual posts.

So how many of these posts should you read? Well, there's no hard and fast answer. What you are trying to do is get a "feel" for the group. You'll quickly notice that some people post a lot more than others. Pay attention to these people. They make up the core of the group and often go a long way toward determining how the group operates. Sometimes you'll notice that these regular posters are split into cliques of one sort or another, and sometimes your first impression will be that these cliques hate each other—at least from the way they are constantly arguing about almost everything. You may even find that you are tempted to join one of these inter-clique battles on one side or another.

Beware. Newsgroups more resemble large, extended families or small villages than any other social organization. And just like families, while they may bicker incessantly amongst themselves, nothing can unite them more quickly than a stranger sticking his nose into the family business.

So do as much research as you can. As the saying goes, "You never get a second chance to make a first impression." To this you might as well add another maxim: "Usenet never forgets."

For proof of this and if you'd like to read the ancient history of any newsgroup, you can go to Google.com's incomprehensibly vast archive of all Usenet posts at http://groups.google.com/googlegro ups/deja_announcement.html and read nearly everything posted to Usenet since 1994.

Toes in the Water: Your First Newsgroup Posts

You've done your homework. You've found a few newsgroups that look promising. You've read their charters and their FAQs. You've read a lot of the older posts, and you've lurked in present time for two or three weeks to make sure you know what's happening on the groups now. You feel like you understand who's who and what's what. You're ready to make your first post.

We can hear you thinking: "Aha! *Now* I get to tell them all about my e-book."

Well, not exactly. No more than you, as a stranger, would walk into a family reunion of two or three hundred people, many of whom have known each other for years, and announce yourself by saying, "Hi, I'm Betty Brash, and I've written this great e-book horror novel called *Dark Blood*, and you have to go read it and buy it *right now*." Unless, of course, you wanted plenty of space around you at the buffet table.

You introduce yourself to a newsgroup the same way you'd introduce yourself to that family reunion. In a word, quietly and calmly—and without the sales pitch.

First, you already have a pitch of sorts in your signature, which is perfectly permissible on Usenet. To begin with, you don't need much more than that.

Your first post should have a subject header something like "Introduction" or "New to group."

Then introduce yourself. "My name is Betty Brash. I've been lurking for a while, and I've decided it's time to come out of the bushes."

Then tell everyone a little about yourself. "I'm a writer, and I'm interested in horror fiction. In fact, I've even written a horror novel that's been published as an e-book. For those interested, there's a link in my sig." ("Sig" is Usenet/e-mail shorthand for "signature.")

Say whatever you want to say, but use common sense. Keep in mind that family reunion analogy. Avoid doing anything to give another user a target, at least until the rest of the group has decided that you're OK.

Usenet Netiquette: Mind Your Manners, and You'll Be Fine

Different cultures have different "right ways of doing things." It's the same with different newsgroups. What's perfectly proper in one group may be anathema in another one, even one that discusses many of the same topics.

However, there are general rules of etiquette that are common to almost all of Usenet, and you should be aware of some of them.

The maximum four-line signature is one such item of netiquette. Another is the rules against spam. There is a third that, while not as hard and fast as the first two, is more often than not a bone of contention. If violated, it is an invitation to flamers, who generally don't need much of an excuse to light up their torches and fire away in any event. This subject is *self-promotion.*

Consider: You are bombarded with commercials and advertising almost, it seems, every waking moment—from your morning newspaper to the radio as you drive to work, the television you watch, the magazines you read, and the Internet and World Wide Web you surf. So if you find yourself at a nice, friendly kaffee-klatsch with several of your neighbors, probably the last thing you'd like to see is one of them suddenly show up tooting a horn and wearing a wooden sandwich board printed in big red letters, "EAT AT JOE'S," even if you know he happens to own Joe's restaurant.

However, if the subject of what you do just happens to come up in conversation, usually people don't mind. Or if the car you drive to the family reunion just happens to have a logo for Joe's restaurant on its side, that also is usually acceptable.

The same approach works on newsgroups. You might post a short announcement about the availability of your e-book every month or so. You'll take a little flack, maybe, but since people already know you from your honest participation in the group, most will be forgiving. Besides, you've already got that signature of yours on every post, right?

And if you should be discussing something with several others (it's called a "discussion thread" in newsgroup-speak) and you hap-

254

pen to mention, in a relevant way, something about your experience with your own e-book, who can say that's not perfectly acceptable?

Nobody will.

Do It Right, and . . .

If you find several newsgroups on the subject of your book, join them, get yourself known and accepted, and restrain your promotional efforts to the methods we've discussed, you may find yourself surprised at the benefits you receive.

As we've noted, you could well be reaching thousands of potential readers, the large majority of whom you'll never know about because they are lurking on the newsgroup. If your participation in the groups has gained you some amount of respect, many of the participants may well be motivated to actually buy your book and mention it to others you've never corresponded with.

The only hint you'll have that this marketing strategy is working is when the sales of your e-book suddenly start to climb. But that would be the best way to find out, wouldn't it?

Start Your Own Newsgroup

What if you just can't find a newsgroup dealing with topics to which your own books might be relevant?

You've got two options: First, find groups you do enjoy and start participating. You'll have to rely on your signature here to get the word out, but once again, even if the topic of the group has little or nothing to do with your book, if you develop a good reputation, people may still be interested in reading your work and use the links in your signature to investigate further.

Or you could start your own newsgroup. On Usenet, this is a fairly long, involved and time-consuming process, and we don't recommend that you pursue it. However, there is a large and growing alternative to Usenet.

Yahoo Groups allows you to quickly and easily set up a Web-based "special interest group" (SIG) on any subject whatsoever. Decide on a discussion topic that would be relevant to the e-books you've written, and then go to http://groups.yahoo.com/start and follow the instructions you find there.

If you like, you can even be so bold as to set up a Yahoo Group devoted to discussing you and your e-books. And, of course, since Yahoo Groups is not a part of Usenet, many of the "netiquette" rules don't really apply or don't apply as strongly. In fact, since you can write the rules for the groups you create, there is nothing stopping you from saying that advertising and promotion of any sort for you own books is perfectly acceptable.

We recommend that you give some thought to setting up your own Yahoo Group. The price—free—is certainly right. It's quite easy to do, even for a novice. You can target the aims of your group very precisely in order to make it a highly effective marketing tool, and besides, you may end up with your own fan club on the World Wide Web.

Just like a "real" author.

But you're already that, aren't you?

Thanks to the amazing power of the digital age and the Internet revolution, yes, you are. Don't let anybody tell you differently.

CHAPTER FORTY-NINE

WRAPPING THINGS UP: A LOOK BACK . . . AND A LOOK AHEAD

The Road You've Taken

For many decades, there has been essentially one road to take if you wanted to publish your book. That road led through bulky paper manuscripts, endless mailings, agents, publishers, contracts, tiny royalties, senseless distribution systems, thousands of bookstores, a handful of powerful book reviewers and all the other sometimes infuriating roadblocks along the way toward becoming a successfully published author.

Worse yet, when many would-be published authors who were not able to negotiate this arduous path examined some of the books that did make it into print, they could be forgiven for coming to the conclusion that chance, luck or maybe even witchcraft sometimes played a larger role in publishing success than talent, skilled craft and hard work.

These were the writers who closed their eyes, clenched their fists and silently pleaded for a chance—just one chance—to put their own books before the public, let others read them, and make up their own minds.

But there really wasn't any way for those authors to do that. If freedom of the press meant the freedom to own one, they were priced out of the market. The highway to publication was a toll road, and almost nobody could afford the fare on their own.

Then, in the early 1990s, all that began to change. A new road appeared, one much less traveled by, and some few hardy literary adventurers took it.

Here Comes the Revolution

Not many people realized it at the time, but that ever-growing collection of computers connected together by telephone cables called the Internet was about to create a new sort of highway called the *information superhighway*. Along those new roads would trundle foot soldiers in the armies of the digital revolution and, just as the soldiers in Gutenberg's armies carried with them a new kind of printing press that vastly expanded the possibilities of creating, publishing and distributing texts over the ancient methods used previously, so did these digital revolutionaries bring with them an even more amazing sort of printing press.

If Gutenberg's invention of movable type dropped the total costs of print by 99 percent over handwritten parchments folios, these digital "presses" lowered the cost of publishing by 999 percent over the printed and bound books that Gutenberg made possible.

Suddenly, for the first time in history, anyone who could afford a cheap computer and a connection to the Internet could publish books that would reach countless readers all over the world.

Now, ten years later, we are living in that digital world, and the revolution is fully upon us. Everything we thought we knew about publishing, everything we've taken for granted about the process, has been turned upside down or done away with entirely.

Your Own Personal Roadmap to the Digital Publishing Age

We would be the last people to try to tell you that this digital revolution is over or even well begun. If there is one thing that characterizes this new era of publishing, one thing that does not change, it is that change is constant.

When we first submitted an outline for this book to our publishers, we intended to mention several creation and delivery technologies that were then current in electronic publishing. But by the time, a few months later, we began to write the manuscript for the book you now hold in your hand, at least 20 percent of what we'd planned to discuss had either changed so much as to be no longer recognizable or vanished entirely.

Here are some examples:

We'd planned to talk about the Glassbook Reader. But before we could, the Glassbook was bought by Adobe and subsumed into the .pdf world of Adobe eBook Reader.

We'd intended to discuss a pair of stand-alone, handheld electronic book readers called the Rocket eBook and the SoftBook. Yet even as we tussled with that first outline, both of the companies making those machines were bought by the Gemstar Corporation and transmogrified into Gemstar and RCA's Reb 1100 and Reb 1200 machines.

As we wrote this book, at least three new e-book reading computers have been announced, some of them offering new features and conveniences not yet seen.

Dozens of new e-publishers have sprung up. Hundreds, perhaps thousands, of e-books have been published. And court cases, some of them critical to the future of e-publishing, have made headlines all over the world.

In spite of all this—no, *because* of all this—we are reasonably certain that even this book will have errors in it by the time it is published and you read it. Most of the errors will be of fact, of references to formats that have suddenly appeared or equally suddenly vanished; to companies that dissolved and new companies that opened for business; but most especially, to new technologies of e-publishing.

Trying to describe all the processes of e-publishing today, let alone in the near future, is somewhat akin to the blind men who tried to puzzle out an elephant—except in our case, the elephant is running down the digital superhighway at a thousand miles per hour.

This continual change in e-publishing is the reason we've structured this book as we have. There are many other books that cover this subject with great attention to minute and specific detail. Sadly, almost all of these books were in large part hopelessly obsolete within a short time of their publication, sometimes even earlier.

But the path of the Internet, the World Wide Web and e-publishing itself need not be totally opaque. Even something as recently arrived as the digital age does have a history, a track record, that functions much as do the banks of a river: The river may shift and flow wildly, speed up, slow down or carve new channels, but mostly the banks that have constrained it will continue to do so. We have tried to give you a feel for the banks that have grown up around the digital torrent, so that even if specific steps have changed by the time you read this book, you will be able to figure out most of the new twists and turns for yourself.

Usenet newsgroups were around for a long time before the World Wide Web made an appearance, and they were structured in certain ways for a reason. Those structures still remain, though Usenet is a million times larger than it was in those days. And though the concept of newsgroups itself has now shifted in some part onto the Web, with places like Yahoo Groups, much of the original Usenet paradigm has shifted right along with it. Twenty years ago people put information into their e-mail and newsgroup signatures. They still do today, and the loose set of rules governing signatures, first enunciated in netiquette so old hardly anyone remembers its origins, still apply.

The basic paradigm remains in force: The digital world is a *connected* world where you can move information freely from one side of the globe to the other with the touch of a key or the click of a mouse. That one simple fact is at the heart of e-publishing, and it will remain so. The rest is just detail.

The Future Is Now . . . Sort Of

W.T. Quick, one of the authors of this book, is a full-blown computer geek. OK, that's me, and I'm going to step out from behind the editorial, collaborative, maybe even imperial "we" to tell you a little story.

I have a home office with several computers wired together in a local area network. Some of the computers are connected by cables. But others, especially my laptop, are connected to the rest wirelessly, using radio waves.

This means that I can wander about with my laptop anywhere within the range of the radio transmitter (a few hundred feet) while connected with my other computers as well as to the Internet.

My laptop is small but powerful. It weighs less than three pounds and is about the same weight and general size as a thick hardcover book—say, John Grisham's latest opus.

I have several e-book reader programs installed on this machine, including the Adobe eBook Reader, one feature of which allows the user to turn the viewing area from horizontal to vertical. This means I can open up the laptop, hold it like a book and read text on the screen, which is now to the left. The text covers just about the same space as a page in a standard print hardcover.

Recently, I lay in bed late at night, reading an e-book on this little machine. It was easy, simple, and after a bit of experience, as natural as reading a "real" book—with a few advantages that "real" books couldn't offer. For instance, if I ran across a word whose definition I didn't know, I could simply click on that word and a dictionary would pop up with the definition. Also, because the screen was backlit, I could read my e-book in a totally darkened room. One of the features of the Adobe eBook Reader is a button you can click on that will take you directly to an online bookstore that sells e-books in Adobe format—in this case, at bn.com.

I finished the book I was reading, decided I wanted to read something new, and so I clicked on the bookstore icon. Since I was already wirelessly connected to the Internet via a high-speed DSL connection, almost instantly a page appeared on my screen at the bn.com online site. I checked out the science fiction section, looking for anything interesting.

As I scrolled through a list of several hundred books, something caught my eye: It was my own name . . . next to the title of my first published print novel, a book that has been long out of print.

It's hard to explain my excitement. This book, my first, has remained one of my favorites, and I was saddened when it was no longer available. I'd arranged to have the book e-published but hadn't been notified that the work had actually been issued. Yet here it was!

I clicked on the book, paid for it with a credit card, downloaded it to my laptop, opened it in Adobe eBook Reader and began to read.

At that moment, I felt as if I were in the middle of a miracle. And perhaps I was. I'll be the first to admit that my technical setup is a bit advanced over that of the average computer user's, but . . .

In five years, maybe less, many, many people will connect to the Internet with small "information appliances" the same way I do now. And the world will change, not just for e-publishers, but for everyone.

And your e-book, just like mine, will be in that new world forever.

Wrapping Things Up: A Look Back . . . and a Look Ahead

RESOURCES

E-Publishers

e-reads.com

E-publisher founded by Richard Curtis. Huge stock of formerly print-published e-books.

www.ereads.com

eBookAd.com

Major portal for e-books, information and news. Excellent search engine.

www.ebookad.com

atRandom

Random House online venture.

www.randomhouse.com/atrandom/

Online Lists of E-Publishers

eBooks-n-Bytes

Maintains a large list of e-publishers, along with a thumbnail write-up on each house. The write-ups offer concise, worthwhile information.

www.ebooksnbytes.com/epub_list.html

eBook Palace

Lists thirty-nine e-publishers with links and brief commentary. An added twist: The number of visits from eBook PaLace's Web site to each e-publisher's Web site is noted.
www.ebooksearchengine.com/cgi-bin/ebooks/
ebooks.cgi?search = CAT&Category = ebook%20Publishers

Major Online Bookstores

Amazon.com
www.amazon.com
Barnes & Noble
www.bn.com or www.barnesandnoble.com
Borders
www.borders.com or www.amazon.com

Text Editing and Word Processing Software

Microsoft Word
www.microsoft.com/word
Corel WordPerfect
www3.corel.com/cgi-bin/gx.cgi/AppLogic+FTContentServer
?pagename=Corel/Product/
Details&id=CC11NDB84AC
StarOffice StarWriter
www.sun.com/software/star/staroffice/5.2/whatsnew/
writer.html

File Compression Utilities

Winzip
www.winzip.com
PKZip
www.pkware.com
Diffuse Project: Guide to Compression Formats
www.diffuse.org/zip.html

HTML Editors

Microsoft FrontPage

   www.microsoft.com/frontpage/

SoftQuad HoTMetaL PRO

   www.hotmetalpro.com

Netscape Composer

   http://home.netscape.com/communicator/composer/v4.0/

Adobe GoLive

   www.adobe.com/products/golive/

HTML Information

WWW Consortium

   www.w3.org/MarkUp/Guide/

National Center for Supercomputing Applications

   www.ncsa.uiuc.edu/General/Internet/WWW/HTMLPrimer.html

Webmonkey

   http://hotwired.lycos.com/webmonkey/authoring/html_basics/

CD-ROM Software and Hardware

Adaptec Corporation

   www.adaptec.com

Hewlett-Packard

   www.hpcdwriter.com/products/internal_cdwriter.asp

E-Book Software Readers

Microsoft Reader

   www.microsoft.com/reader/default.asp

Adobe eBook Reader

   www.adobe.com/products/ebookreader/main.html

E-Book Software Tools

Microsoft Reader File Format Creator

   www.microsoft.com/ebooks/tools/make_authors.asp

eBookExpress (Web-based Microsoft Reader File Creator)
www.ebookexpress.com

Adobe PDF File Format Creator/Converter
www.adobe.com/products/acrobat/main.html

Win2PDF (PDF Converter)
www.daneprairie.com

PrintToPDF (PDF Conversion for the Mac)
www.jwwalker.com

Adobe Web-Based PDF Converter
http://createpdf.adobe.com

E-Book Hardware Readers

Gemstar eBook Readers
www.ebook-gemstar.com/eb_dev/index.htm

hiebook eBook Reader
www.ebookad.com/hiebook/

Open E-Book Format

www.openebook.org/index.htm

Associate Advertising Program

iBoost.com
www.iboost.com/profit/advertising/articles/06018.htm

Donation-Funded Web Sites

Andrew Sullivan
www.andrewsullivan.com

Mickey Kaus
www.kausfiles.com

Joshua Micah Marshall's Talking Points
http://j-marshall.com/talk/

Payment System Sites

PayPal

    www.paypal.com

Amazon.com honor system

    https://secure.paypal.com/cgi-bin/webscr?cmd=_web-tools

Web Sites for Writers

Writer's Digest Books

    www.writersdigest.com

Malone Editorial Services (Susan Malone)

    www.maloneeditorial.com

Science Fiction and Fantasy Writers of America, Inc.

    Contains a wealth of information for writers.

    www.sfwa.org

AuthorLink

    www.authorlink.com

United States Copyright Office

    www.loc.gov/copyright/

ISBN Information

ISBN.org

    www.isbn.org/standards/home/isbn/us/isbnqa.html#Q10

R.R. Bowker

    www.bowker.com

Association of Authors' Representatives

    www.publishersweekly.com/aar/

News and Special Interest Groups

Yahoo Newsgroups

    http://groups.yahoo.com

Google Usenet Newsgroups Searchable Archive

    http://groups.google.com

Public Software Archives

CNET Download.com
   http://download.cnet.com/downloads/
Tucows Software Archives
   www.tucows.com
MacOSArchives for the Macintosh
   www.macosarchives.com
DaveCentral's Linux Archives
   http://linux.davecentral.com

Voice Recognition Software

IBM ViaVoice
   www-4.ibm.com/software/speech/desktop/
Lernout & Hauspie's Voice Xpress
   www.lhsl.com/voicexpress/
Dragon Naturally Speaking
   www.dragonsys.com

Domain Name Search and Information

Network Solutions (Internic)
   www.networksolutions.com

Domain Hosting Information

Web Host Directory
   www.webhostdir.com

Marketing and Internet Marketing Web Site

Web Marketing and E-Commerce Center
   www.wilsonweb.com

E-Book Review Source Lists

eBook Connections
   www.ebookconnections.com

ePublishing Connections
www.epublishingconnections.com

Internet Search Engines

Google
www.google.com
Yahoo
www.yahoo.com
AltaVista
www.altavista.com

General Interest

Project Gutenberg
http://promo.net/pg/
Tim Berners-Lee's Home Page (creator of the World Wide Web)
www.w3.org/People/Berners-Lee/Overview.html

BIBLIOGRAPHY

Moira Anderson Allen, *Writing.com: Creative Internet Strategies to Advance Your Writing Career*, Allworth Press, 1999.

Richard Curtis, *Beyond the Bestseller*, Plume, 1990.

———, *How to Be Your Own Literary Agent*, Houghton Mifflin, 1996.

Vincent Flanders and Michael Willis, *Web Pages That Suck: Learn Good Design by Looking at Bad Design*, Sybex Computer Books, 1988.

Steve Krug and Roger Black, *Don't Make Me Think! A Common Sense Approach to Web Usability*, Que, 2000.

Jay Conrad Levinson, Rick Frishman and Michael Larsen, *Guerrilla Marketing for Writers*, Writer's Digest Books, 2001.

Paul McFedries, *Complete Idiot's Guide to Creating a Web Page, Fourth Edition*, Complete Idiot's Guide, 1999.

Jennifer Niederst, *HTML Pocket Reference (Nutshell Handbook)* O'Reilly & Associates, 1999.

Jennifer Niederst and Richard Koman, *Learning Web Design: A Beginner's Guide to HTML, Graphics, and Beyond*, O'Reilly & Associates, March, 2001.

Jakob Nielsen, *Designing Web Usability: The Practice of Simplicity*, New Riders Publishing, 1999.

Deborah S. Ray and Eric J. Ray, *HTML 4 for Dummies: Quick Reference (For Dummies)*, Hungry Minds, Inc., 2000.

M.J. Rose and Angela Adair-Hoy, *How to Publish and Promote Online*, St. Martin's Griffin, 2001.

Victoria Rosenborg, *ePublishing for Dummies*, IDG Books Worldwide, 2001.

Judy Strauss and Raymond Frost, *Marketing on the Internet: Principles of On-Line Marketing*, Prentice-Hall, 1999.

Anthony Tedesco and Paul Tedesco, *Online Markets for Writers*, Owl Books, 2000.

Index

8961